Coffee, climate change and adaption strategies

for German coffee producers

This bachelor thesis was submitted at Osnabrück University of Applied Sciences in 2015 under the title: „Analysis of the climate change related changes on the global green coffee market for the derivation of procurement strategy alternatives of German coffee producers".

Markus Esser

Coffee, climate change and adaption strategies for German coffee producers

Bibliografische Information der Deutschen Nationalbibliothek:
Die Deutsche Nationalbibliothek verzeichnet diese Publikation in der
Deutschen Nationalbibliografie; detaillierte bibliografische Daten
sind im Internet über http://dnb.dnb.de abrufbar.

Herstellung und Verlag: BoD – Books on Demand, Norderstedt

ISBN: 978-3-7386-3626-0

I   Kurzfassung/Abstract

Kurzfassung

Der Klimawandel und die globale Erwärmung beeinflussen die Anbaubedingungen weltweit. Diese Bachelorarbeit analysiert die durch den Klimawandel hervorgerufenen Entwicklungen auf dem weltweiten Rohkaffeemarkt insbesondere im Hinblick auf den Arabica Kaffee, um daraus Ansätze für deutsche Kaffeeproduzenten abzuleiten um diesen Entwicklungen entgegenzuwirken. In diesem Zusammenhang prognostiziert diese Bachelorarbeit das weltweite Angebot sowie die weltweite Nachfrage für Arabica Kaffee für das Jahr 2050 und zeigt dadurch eine größer werdende Differenz zwischen Angebot und Nachfrage auf. Des Weiteren wird eine Auswahl von Ansätzen dargelegt, die deutsche Kaffeeproduzenten nutzen können, um die Auswirkungen des Klimawandels auf den Arabica Kaffee Anbau zu verringern und das Angebot an Arabica Kaffee abzusichern. Die Arbeit schließt mit dem Ergebnis, dass ein Handeln der deutschen Kaffeeproduzenten nötig ist und gibt einen Vorschlag, wie dies zu realisieren wäre.

Abstract

Climate change and global warming are highly affecting the cultivation conditions worldwide. This bachelor thesis analyses the global warming related changes on the global green coffee market – especially for *C. arabica* – to derivate approaches for German coffee producers to adapt their procurement strategies. In this context this thesis forecasts the worldwide supply and demand for *C. arabica* for the year 2050, which shows a large gap between *C. arabica* supply and demand in 2050 – and presents a limited number of approaches for German coffee producers to reduce the impacts of the climate change and to secure the *C. arabica* supply. This thesis shows that German coffee producers need to act and proposes how this could be realised.

Analysis of the climate change related changes on the global green coffee market for the derivation of procurement strategy alternatives of German coffee producers

Page I

II   Table of Contents

Analysis of the climate change related changes on the global green coffee market for the derivation of procurement strategy alternatives of German coffee producers

Page II

III List of Figures

Analysis of the climate change related changes on the global green coffee market for the derivation of procurement strategy alternatives of German coffee producers

Page IV

IV   List of Tables

Analysis of the climate change related changes on the global green coffee market for the
derivation of procurement strategy alternatives of German coffee producers
Page V

V   Abbreviations

AAGR	Average annual growth rate
C. arabica	Arabica Coffee
C. canephora	Robusta Coffee
CPWW	Coffee Processing Wastewaters
ECF	European Coffee Federation
GCM	Global circulation model
ICO	International Coffee Organisation
IPCC	Intergovernmental Panel on Climate Change
masl	Meters above sea level
RCP	Representative Concentration Pathways
USDA	United States Department of Agriculture
WMO	World Meteorological Organization

1   Introduction

1.1   Context

Coffee can be defined as one of the preferred drinks in the western hemisphere. A large part of the European population consumes coffee products on a daily basis and Oliver Wendell Holmes, an American physician, professor and poet, wrote about coffee „The morning cup of coffee has an exhilaration about it which the cheering influence of the afternoon or evening cup of tea cannot be expected to reproduce"[1]. The daily consumption of the product which has its origins in Ethiopia and is mostly grown in Central and South America as well as Asia is now at risk because of the global climate change[2].

1.2   Relevance

As shown in many studies, the coffee business is a constantly growing one. While the consumption was at 57.9 million 60-kg bags of coffee in 1964, the consumption was at 142.0 million 60-kg bags in the year 2012. This leads to an average annual growth rate (AAGR) of 1.9 %[3]. But whilst the coffee demand is growing constantly, the production is highly volatile due to unstable impacts like the weather. [4]

Germany with a net-import of 23.613 million 60-kg bags in 2012/13, as it is focussed in this dissertation, is the second largest coffee importing country behind the United States with a net-import of 42.305 million 60-kg bags. But the German imports are not only used for consumption, Germany has the largest re-export volume worldwide. Between 2000 and 2011 Germany was responsible for 46.2 % of the world's re-exports of green coffee, 21.9 % of

[1] Holmes, Sr. 1891, p. 1
[2] Bunn et al. 2014a, pp. 98–99
[3] International Coffee Organisation (ICO) 2013a, p. 10.
[4] Camargo, Ângelo paes de, Camargo, Marcelo Bento Paes de 2001, p. 67.

roasted coffee and 18.8 % of soluble coffee. This indicates that nearly half of the German import is re-exported. [5]

Besides the western hemisphere also the coffee market in Asia is growing. Behind Japan with its 8.4 million 60-kg bags in 2013, China- with an AAGR over 12 %- is getting more and more attention on the global coffee market[6]. If China maintains this growth rate, the consumption can reach 2.8 million 60-kg bags in 2020 which would boost China into the top ten of coffee consuming countries[7]. This assumption is also backed by the statements made on the Africa Fine Coffee Conference in February 2015 which implicate that the demand is likely to rise by almost 25 % in the next five years due to an increasing westernisation of the societies in India, China and Latin America[8].

Summarised, it can be said that the demand of coffee will grow within the next decades. However, the production of the green coffee is at risk because of the global climate change. The *C. arabica* plant (Arabica Coffee) which is responsible for approximately 55 % of the worldwide coffee production is a very sensitive plant. An average temperature increase of two degrees in the growing areas in combination with more frequently extreme weather events can lead to mayor crop losses. [9, 10] This scenario will almost certainly occur and therefore it will be reviewed in this dissertation. But as plants of the *C. canephora* coffee (Robusta Coffee) are better adapted to slightly higher temperatures and less affected by the climate changes the dissertation will mainly focus on the *C. arabica*[11]. In 2014/2015 55 % of the worldwide produced coffee is expected to be *C. arabica* coffee but this share is expected to decline in the future[12]. This

---

[5] International Coffee Organisation (ICO) 2013a, p. 29.
[6] International Coffee Organisation (ICO) 2015c, p. 1
[7] International Coffee Organisation (ICO) 2013b, p. 9.
[8] Bariyo 2015, p. 1.
[9] Haggar, Schepp 2012, pp. 7–8.
[10] United States Department of Agriculture (USDA) 2014b, p. 1.
[11] Haggar, Schepp 2012, pp. 4–5.
[12] United States Department of Agriculture (USDA) 2014b, p. 1.

___

will have a considerable impact on the coffee producers within the EU as *C. arabica* accounted for 62.8 % of all coffee imports in 2013[13].

1.3   Synopsis

The goal of this dissertation is to analyse the climate predictions, crop growing indices and the estimated coffee demand for 2050 under consideration of the climate change related impacts to derive procurement strategy alternatives for German coffee producers. With this purpose, the second chapter contains a literature review to introduce the reader into the current status of the global green coffee production, the global green coffee demand, the importance of coffee for the EU and Germany and into climate change, its general impact and the global warming, which is the driving determinant in this issue. Furthermore, the second chapter of this thesis exemplarily focuses on the development of the Mexican green coffee production till 2050 considering the climate change impact and also indicates the climate change related coffee suitability changes until 2050. The third chapter comprises the methodology and which methods and formulas were used for forecasting the supply and the demand. Chapter four is divided in two parts. The first part presents and analyses the results of the calculations, the second part presents environmental, economic and social sustainable approaches. The fifth chapter concludes the outcome of the calculations and gives recommendations for German coffee producers which actions they should take to adapt their procurement strategies. The following sixth and last chapter contains the discussion about the thesis.

___

[13] European Coffee Federation (ECF) 2014, p. 10.

2   Literature Review

2.1   Coffee introduction

As already mentioned in the context, coffee has its origins in Ethiopia. By the 15th century coffee was being cultivated in Yemen and being exported to India in the late 1600's by the Dutch. In 1699 some plants where shipped to Batavia in Java, in what is now Indonesia and within a few years the Dutch colonies had become the main supplier of coffee to Europe. In 1720 a French naval officer shipped the first coffee plant to his post in Martinique which laid the basis for a new cash crop that could be grown in the New World but it was the Dutch who first started the spread of the coffee plants in Central and South America. By the 1830's Brazil was the world's largest producer of green coffee with about 600,000 60-kg bags a year which is just a drop in the ocean compared to the actual production of over 50 million 60-kg bags in crop year 2012/2013. And with this many bags Brazil is still the world's largest producer of green coffee and stands for 35 % green coffee worldwide. By now the importance of coffee and coffee products to the world economy cannot be overstated. It is one of the most valuable primary products in world trade and in many years second in value only to oil as a source of foreign exchange to producing countries. Only the worldwide exported green coffee in 2012/2013 was at 100.7 million 60-kg bags (6.04 million tons) worth US$ 19.2 billion. In comparison, the amount of harvested tea in 2012 was at 4.68 million tons and was worth US$ 11.3 billion. The overall value of all coffee products can be estimated a lot higher so it's no wonder that its cultivation, processing, trading, transportation and marketing provides employment for hundreds of millions of people worldwide, especially in many of the world's Least Developed Countries.[14, 15, 16, 17, 18]

---

[14] Deutscher Kaffeeverband 2013, p. 3
[15] Deutscher Kaffeeverband 2014
[16] Food and Agriculture Organization of the United States (FAO) 2014
[17] International Coffee Organisation (ICO) 2015d, pp. 1–2.
[18] International Tea Committee 2014

2.2   Global production and demand now and in the future

The world production of 2013/2014 is revised up from June estimated by 2.4 to 152.2 million 60-kg bags. This is mostly influenced by three mayor countries. Columbia raised from 11.0 million to 12.1 million 60-kg bags within the last year, Brazil is enhanced from 43.7 million to 54.5 million 60-kg bags due to higher *C. canephora* yield and Vietnam is nearly 900,000 60-kg bags higher at 29.8 million due to area expansion. [19]

The steady decline in prices seems to reflect the imbalance between supply and demand due to an excess of production over consumption. The downward trend started when total production was slightly below world consumption in 2010/2011. [20] Consequently, the total exports during the year reached a record volume of 111.1 million 60-kg bags, stockpiling stocks in both importing and exporting countries[21].

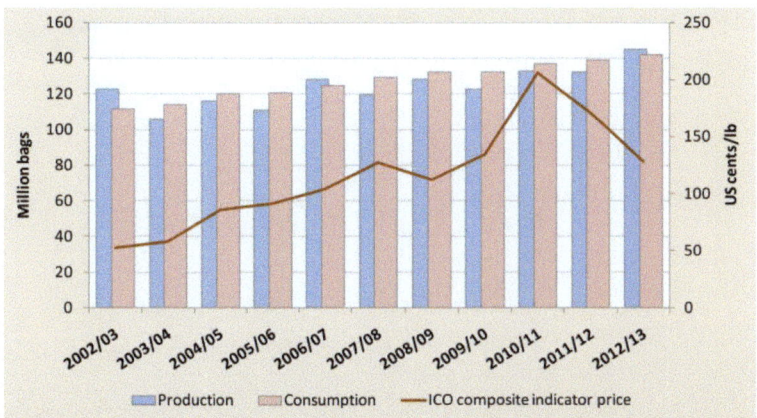

Figure 1: Production, consumption and ICO indicator prices Coffee years 2002/03 to 2012/13[22]

---

[19] United States Department of Agriculture (USDA) 2014b.
[20] International Coffee Organisation (ICO) 2013a, p. 7.
[21] International Coffee Organisation (ICO) 2013a, p. 5.
[22] International Coffee Organisation (ICO) 2013a, p. 7.

But despite the production record level of 111.1 million 60-kg bags in 2012/2013, the total value is estimated at US$ 19 billion. That is a fall of 18 % compared to US$ 23.2 billion in 2011/2012 with 107.7 million 60-kg bags. [23]
In 2013/14 world exports rose back up to 104.8 million 60-kg bags. The main drivers were a strong U.S. and European demand. [24]

As pictured in the figure below the world consumption from 2009 to 2012 has shown a constant upward trend: 142 million 60-kg bags in calendar year 2012 compared to 139 million 60-kg bags in 2011. As the figures indicate the main drivers are the emerging markets who had an AAGR of 3.9 % and the exporting countries itself who had an AAGR of 2.4 % over the four years while the AAGR of the traditional markets was at 0.8 %. If the growth of world consumption continues, the ratio of global supply and consumption will tighten again which will lead to a rise in the coffee-prices, again. [25] The world consumption for 2013/2014 is lowered back to 142.4 million 60-kg bags after the consumption of the EU is revised down 3.2 million 60-kg bags to 42.6 million 60-kg bags[26].

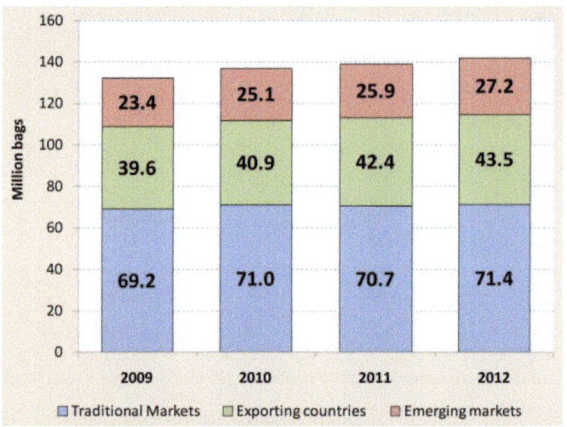

Figure 2: World Consumption Calendar years 2009 to 2012[27]

[23] International Coffee Organisation (ICO) 2013a, p. 9.
[24] United States Department of Agriculture (USDA) 2014b, p. 4.
[25] International Coffee Organisation (ICO) 2013a, p. 10.
[26] United States Department of Agriculture (USDA) 2014b, p. 4.
[27] International Coffee Organisation (ICO) 2013a, p. 10.

As it can be seen on the previous page, the forecast of global production for 2014/2015 went down to 149.8 million 60-kg bags. And as it can be seen below, the world *C. arabica* production is expected to decline again while *C. canephora* is expected to rise. This will shrink *C. arabica's* dominance down to 55 %[28].

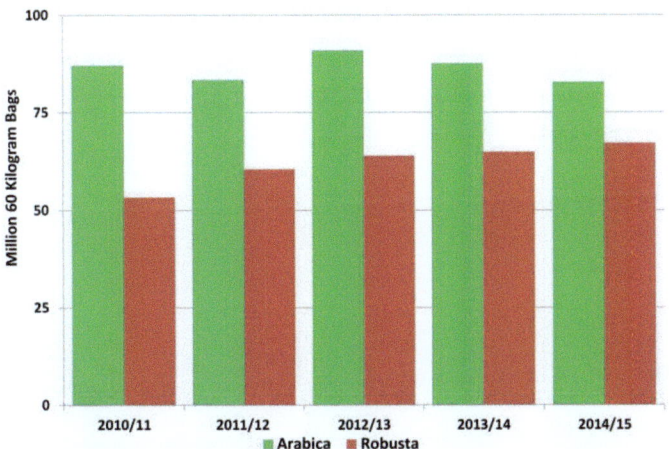

Figure 3: World Arabica and Robusta Coffee Production Converging[29]

Ross Colbert, an analyst of the Rabobank writes about the growth of coffee: „Continued growth in global coffee will be driven by three key drivers: innovation in single cup brewing (e.g. K-Cups, pods, etc.); premiumisation, with consumers choosing to drink higher quality coffee; and increased consumption in the 'away-from-home' channel in developed markets, led by Starbucks and McDonald's."[30]. But not only is the growth of the developed markets influencing the global growth of demand. Also undeveloped markets can change the global demand of coffee.

One of the markets that has the potential to change the demand significantly is China. As Japan, China is a traditional tea-drinking country with a culture that

---

[28] United States Department of Agriculture (USDA) 2014b, p. 1.
[29] United States Department of Agriculture (USDA) 2014b, p. 1.
[30] Colbert 2013, p. 2.

reaches back for centuries. However, annual consumption of coffee in Japan in the late 1960s was nearly at the same level as the consumption in China is right now, and Japans consumption accelerated to exceed 7 million 60-kg bags since 2004 and is now the fourth largest coffee consuming country. This similar condition raises questions as how Chinas development will affect the coffee industry. But besides the questions it can clearly be said, that the demand in China is rising rapidly. In the last 15 years China had an AAGR of 12.8 % and the consumption rose from 199,000 60-kg bags in 1998 to around 1.1 million 60-kg bags in 2012. [31, 32]

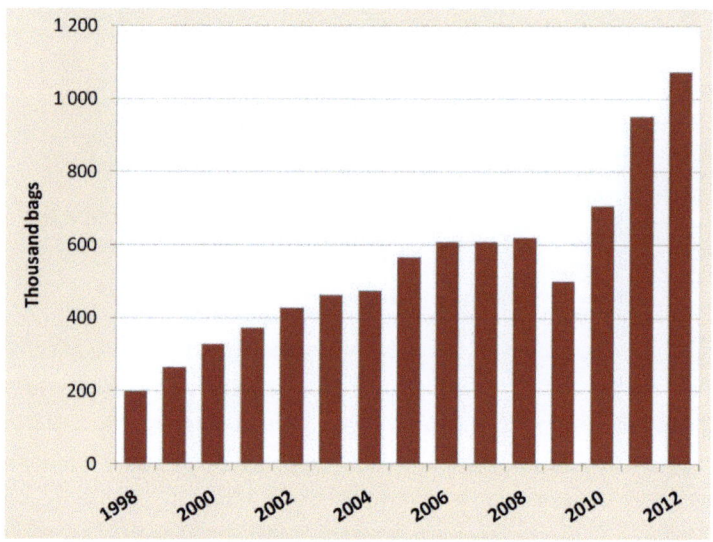

Figure 4: Coffee consumption in China 1998 to 2012[33]

Despite the strong potential, the absolute level of consumption remains low. Even if China reaches 2.8 million 60-kg bags by 2020, the per capita consumption would only be around 125 grams, compared to 4.84 kg in Western

[31] International Coffee Organisation (ICO) 2013a, p. 30.
[32] International Coffee Organisation (ICO) 2013b, pp. 8–11.
[33] International Coffee Organisation (ICO) 2013a, p. 30.

Europe. Also, the opening up of investment opportunities, particularly in the roasting industry, can help to influence consumer habits. Indeed western coffee brands which are active in China since the 1980s have changed the coffee culture. While the instant coffee segment is under control of Nestle (Switzerland) and Mondelez (U.S.), the freshly-brewed segment is mostly controlled by Starbucks (U.S.), Barista Coffee (Taiwan) and Blenz (Canada). For Starbucks, China was the second biggest market in 2014 and Starbucks aims to raise up the number of their stores to 1500 in 2015. This success also attracts other competitors like Caffe Bene (South Korea), who wants to open over 5,000 stores till the end of 2015. Based on this data, the China Coffee Association Beijing expects an AAGR between 15 and 20 %. But the investments are not just limited to the point of sale. Nestle opened a Nescafé Coffee Center in the Pu´er Industrial Park in Yunnan and Volcafe, a part of ED&F Man (United Kingdom), is in a Joint Venture with the Chinese coffee-exporter Simao Arabicasm Coffee Co.[34, 35, 36] In summary it can be anticipated, that the global green coffee demand will rise and that developing countries like China will be the driving force.

2.3   Importance of coffee for Europe and Germany

According to the United States Department of Agriculture (USDA) the European Union accounts for nearly half of world green coffee imports. The main suppliers are Vietnam (24 %), Brazil (20 percent) and Indonesia (6 %). The consumption in the EU is expected to rise to 45.7 million 60-kg bags in the next year. [37] As stated by the European Coffee Federation (ECF), the overall import ratio *C. arabica/c. canephora* for Europe has shifted fractionally towards *C. arabica* from 62.4 % in 2012 to 62.8 % in 2013[38].

---

[34] International Coffee Organisation (ICO) 2013a, p. 30.
[35] International Coffee Organisation (ICO) 2013b, pp. 8–11.
[36] Stefanie Schmitt 2015, pp. 1–2.
[37] United States Department of Agriculture (USDA) 2014b, p. 3.
[38] European Coffee Federation (ECF) 2014, p. 10.

Within the EU, Germany is not only one of the countries with the largest import, it also had the highest total consumption in the last years.

Table 1: Total coffee consumption in thousand 60-kg bags [39]

	2010/11	2011/12	2012/13
European Union	40,700	40,575	41,630
Germany	9,057	9,057	8,777

The second and third most consuming countries where France and Italy with fluctuating consumptions between 5,571 and 6,023 thousand 60-kg bags. Besides the highest total consumption Germany also has a high per capita consumption which stayed quite stable in the last years. [40]

Table 2: Per capita coffee consumption in kg [41]

	2010/11	2011/12	2012/13
European Union	4.89	4.82	4.84
Germany	6.72	6.85	6.40

The country in the EU with the highest per capita consumption is Luxembourg with a per capita consumption between 24 and 27.5 kg, which is likely caused by important volumes of coffee purchased by tourists and border region inhabitants. Such purchases are not included in the statistic because a false impression of the volume consumed locally would be given. [42]

Not only is the consumption in Germany at a large scale, also are the production of coffee products and the re-export which makes Germany to world's largest coffee re-exporting country. In the years between 2000 and 2011 Germany's re-exports reached an average annual level of 8.6 million 60-kg bags, accounting for 28.1 % of the world's total re-exports. This also indicates that the re-exports of Germany account for 48.3 percent of average annual imports of 17.7 million 60-kg bags. The main destinations where the United States,

---

[39] European Coffee Federation (ECF) 2014, p. 21.
[40] European Coffee Federation (ECF) 2014, p. 21.
[41] European Coffee Federation (ECF) 2014, p. 21.
[42] European Coffee Federation (ECF) 2014, pp. 21–22.

Poland, Austria, the Netherlands and France. In total Germany was responsible for 46.2 % of the worldwide green coffee re-exports, 21.9 % of roasted coffee and 18.8 % of soluble coffee during that period. [43, 44, 45] And while the volume increased, also the value increased as it can be seen on the next page.

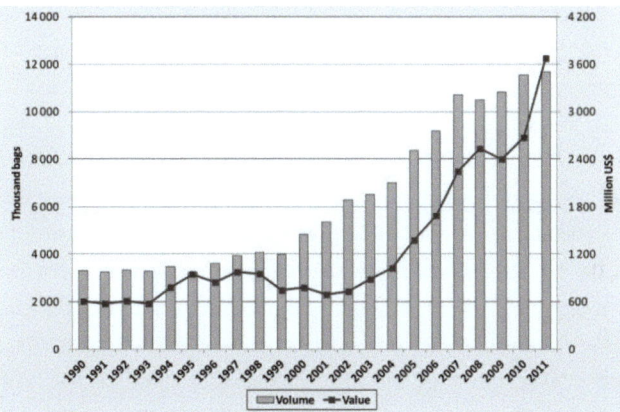

Figure 5: Volume and value of re-exports of all forms of coffee by Germany (1990 to 2011)[46]

Not only the German economy but also the German government profits greatly from coffee. Only in 2015 the German government earned 1.05 billion Euro in taxes. The highest income in taxes where ascertained in 1994, where the government earned over 1.16 billion Euro. The income in taxes is on this level because Germany claims special taxes for coffee products. The tax rate for roasted coffee amounts 2.13 Euro per kilo while the tax rate for soluble coffee amounts 4.78 Euro per kilo. Also coffee-containing products are taxed when imported to Germany according to their coffee-percentage. [47, 48] The coffee related companies in Germany are organized in the German Coffee Foundation which hosts about 150 members. Most of the companies are small and medium-

---

[43] Hammer 2013, p. 1.
[44] International Coffee Organisation (ICO) 2013a, p. 29.
[45] International Coffee Organisation (ICO) 2013c, p. 6.
[46] International Coffee Organisation (ICO) 2013c, p. 8.
[47] Hammer 2013, p. 1.
[48] International Coffee Organisation (ICO) 2013a, p. 29.

sized enterprises, which have the same right of co-determination as the large companies. [49, 50]

2.4   Climate change and the general impact

The air, water and ground of our planet Earth are all linked to its atmosphere through the exchange of gases. These processes are one of the biggest factors in determining Earth's climate or 'average weather'. Over the history of the Earth, the climate has constantly changed but in the last 50-100 years the changes elevated and happened much faster than the planet has seen in the recorded history of humans. According to the Asian Development Bank the broad consensus of the IPCC (Intergovernmental Panel on Climate Change), made up by expert scientists from among 195 countries is that: *"Warming of the climate system is in no doubt, and since the 1950s, many of the observed changes are unprecedented over decades to millennia ['000 years]."* They also say that it is "extremely likely" that the human activities have been the dominant causes of the acceleration of the warming during this time and that climate change is responsible for significant challenges for our way of life on Earth. [51] "The relatively recent expansion of human populations and activities through industrialization, agricultural development, deforestation and the burning of fossil fuels such as oil, gas and coal, have released much higher quantities of Greenhouse Gases and at a much faster rate than natural processes alone. This has the impact of disrupting the natural balance of atmospheric gases, increased heat-trapping and warming of the Earth's surface (ground and sea). Because gases distributed through large-scale atmospheric circulation, the heat-trapping affects the whole planet and is called *'global warming'* - the major driving factor in man-made climate change." [52]

---

[49] Deutscher Kaffeeverband 2015b, pp. 1–2
[50] Deutscher Kaffeeverband 2015a, pp. 1–9
[51] Asian Development Bank (ADB) 2013, p. 1.
[52] Asian Development Bank (ADB) 2013, pp. 1–2.

The IPCC estimates that the increase in average global temperatures will be between 1.8 °C to 4.0 °C by the end of the 21st century. Compared to this in the last 100 years (1906-2005) the global temperature increased by an average of 0.74 °C (+0.56 °C to 0.92 °C) but this appears to have accelerated since the 1970s.The evidence from coffee farmers of numerous coffee growing regions is that they are already suffering from the influences of the increased temperature. Precise modelling of the influence of climate change for either *C. arabica* or *C. canephora* is limited. [53] Also according to the Fourth Assessment Report of the World Meteorological Organization (WMO), semi-arid and sub-humid regions of Africa, Asia and Latin America are likely to heat up during this century and freshwater availability is going to decrease[54]. As an example, the air temperature in the tropical areas of Brazil the air temperature is supposed to increase 1.1 °C to 6.4 °C[55]. The following figures 6 and 7 are visualising the previous and predicted surface temperature changes to illustrate and clarify the direction of the development.

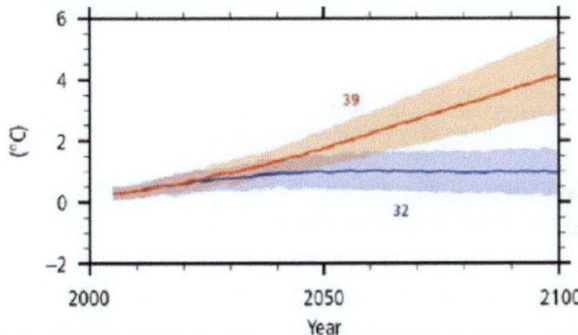

Figure 6: Global average surface temperature change until 2100 (relative to 1986-2005)[56]

[53] Davis et al. 2012, pp. 1–2.
[54] World Meteorological Organization (WMO) 2008, p. 6.
[55] Camargo, Marcelo Bento Paes de 2010, p. 241.
[56] Pachauri, Meyer 2013, p. 62.

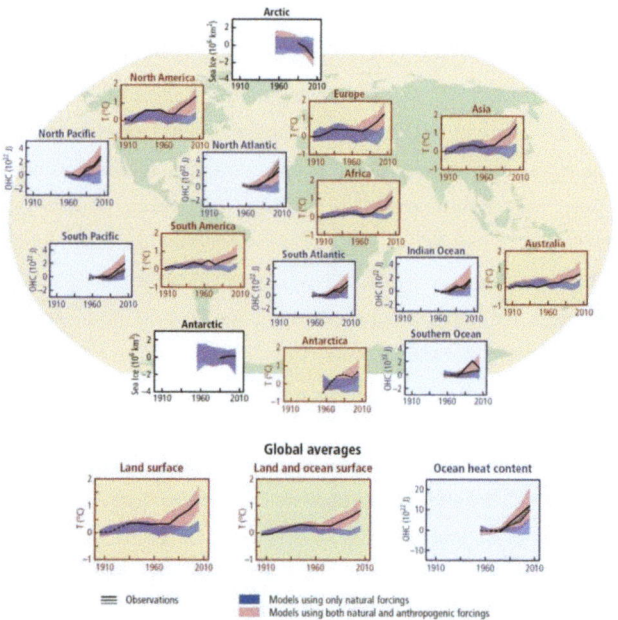

Figure 7: Comparison of observed and simulated change in continental surface temperatures on land (yellow panels), Arctic and Antarctic September sea ice extent (white panels), and upper ocean heat content in the major ocean basins (blue panels)[57]

The global warming/climate change brings several key risks. Some are more focused on the people living in the affected areas like risks of severe ill-health and disrupted livelihoods through extreme weather events like flooding, systematic risks concerning the infrastructure networks and critical services as well as risks of water and food insecurity, loss of rural livelihoods and income. The risk that threatens the coffee plants is the risk of loss of ecosystems, biodiversity and ecosystem goods, functions and services. [58]

The relationship between the climatic parameters and the coffee production are quite complex, as the environmental factors are affecting the growth and the plants development during the different phonological stages of the crop. [59]

---

[57] Pachauri, Meyer 2013, p. 50.
[58] Pachauri, Meyer 2013, p. 69.
[59] Camargo, Ângelo paes de, Camargo, Marcelo Bento Paes de 2001, p. 67.

Agro-meteorological models predicting the growth, development and productivity can supply information for the soil water monitoring and yield forecast based on the air temperature and water stress derived by a water balance during different crop growth stages, quantifying the effect of the available soil water on the decrease of the final yield. The processes of photosynthesis become limited when water stress occurs, due to closing of the stoma and reduction in other physiological activities in the plant. Other climatic factors can reduce the productivity, such as adverse air temperatures during different growth stages. [60]

According to different sources the optimum temperature range for *C. arabica* coffee is from 14 to 28 °C, from 18 to 21 °C and from 18 to 23 °C[61, 62, 63]. The Food and Agriculture Organization of the United States (FOA) has published following data about the *C. arabica* and *C. canephora* coffee:

	Arabica				Robusta			
	Optimal		Absolute		Optimal		Absolute	
	Min.	Max.	Min.	Max.	Min.	Max.	Min.	Max.
Temperature	14	28	10	34	20	30	12	36
Rainfall	1,400	2,400	750	4,200	1,700	3,000	900	4,000
Soil pH	5.5	7	4.3	8.4	5	6.3	4	8

Figure 8: Optimal and absolute growing conditions for Arabica and Robusta coffee[64]

But despite the disagreement on the temperatures all sources stated consistently that temperatures above the optimum hinder the development and ripening of cherries, reduce growth of the leaves and the plants itself and may cause abortion of flowers on the *C. arabica* coffee plants. All these impacts are leading to loss of quality and needs to be prevented. Additionally, a not well-understood factor is the response of coffee to increased CO_2 concentration

---

[60] Camargo, Marcelo Bento Paes de 2010, p. 240.
[61] Camargo, Marcelo Bento Paes de 2010, p. 241.
[62] DaMatta, Ramalho, José D. Cochicho, pp. 56–57.
[63] Haggar, Schepp 2012, pp. 4–5.
[64] Haggar, Schepp 2012, p. 9.

which will also occur but as there is not much tangible information it won't be considered in this thesis. Nevertheless, increasing mean and maximum temperatures as well as changing distribution of rainfall are expected and certainly will affect coffee production. In addition to these changes the plantations will be affected by more severe and frequently occurring extreme weather events like droughts, tropical storms and heavy winds. Scientific research already showed that many of the current coffee growing regions are already suffering under these changing conditions. [65, 66, 67]

The temperature and rainfall development also has an impact on coffee-related pests and diseases as it increases the altitudinal range in which the fungal disease coffee rust (Hemileia vastatrix) and the coffee berry borer (Hypothenemus hampei) are able to survive. The already affected areas have gradually increased over the past decades, and today, the only effective pesticide is Endosulfan, which poses a health risk to the farmers who apply it. [68, 69]

2.5   Mexican situation now

Mexico with its 1,943,945 sq km of land is located in North America, bordering the United States in the north and Guatemala in the South[70]. The agriculture in Mexico is responsible for 3.6 % of the total GDP and 13.4 % of the total labor force[71, 72]. The cropping of coffee just accounts for a small part of this. As stated on the Country Data Sheet of the ICO (International Coffee Organisation) in 2011 (Appendix 1), coffee is responsible for 0.8 % of the GDP and also for 0.26 % of the exported goods, which are worth over US$ 900 million (Mexico exported 2.1 million 60-kg bags of *C. arabica* coffee and 28 thousand 60-kg bags of *C. canephora* coffee). The main states which are accountable for the

---

[65] DaMatta, Ramalho, José D. Cochicho, pp. 56–57.
[66] Camargo, Marcelo Bento Paes de 2010, p. 241.
[67] Haggar, Schepp 2012, pp. 4–5.
[68] Schroth et al. 2009, p. 616.
[69] Läderach et al. 2013, p. 1.
[70] Central Intelligence Agency (CIA) 2014, p. 1.
[71] Central Intelligence Agency (CIA) 2014, p. 7.
[72] Central Intelligence Agency (CIA) 2014, p. 8.

coffee production in Mexico are Chiapas and Veracruz. Chiapas, which is the biggest coffee producing state in Mexico, is located in the south of Mexico, bordering Guatemala and the Pacific Ocean. Especially the Sierra Madre de Chiapas, which is a largely forested mountain chain, produces about 20 % of the coffee in Chiapas and is one of Mexico's most important coffee regions. This results out of the geographical location and the altitude, which allows a large-scale coffee cultivation. For example in mid-elevation areas (600–1400 meters above sea level, masl), coffee locally covers up to 98 % of the land. Altogether there are 265,400 ha of land highly suitable for *C. arabica* coffee (>60 %), 524,600 ha with a suitability between 60 % and 49 % and over 1.57 million ha of low suitable land for *C. arabica* coffee (<40 %). Besides that the Sierra Madre is also a major water catchment area for surrounding towns and agricultural plains and is characterized by high biodiversity and species endemicity, hosting over 2000 species of plants and at least 600 species of animals. [73, 74, 75]

Veracruz, which is north of Chiapas, is the state with the second largest coffee production in Mexico. The combined agriculture in Veracruz generates 7.9 % of the states GDP and provides 31.7 % of all jobs in this region. The coffee production contributes significantly to these numbers. As in Chiapas the majority of the cultivated coffee is *C. arabica* which is presented by the types Typica, Bourbon, Caturra, Garnica and Mundo Novo. [76] In the 1992 Coffee Census it was revealed that 153,000 ha were devoted to coffee production[77]. But as the Mexican coffee output has grown in the last two decades it can be expected to be far more than that.

[73] Gay et al. 2006, p. 264.
[74] Schroth et al. 2009, p. 614.
[75] Schroth et al. 2009.
[76] Gay et al. 2006, pp. 261+263.
[77] Gay et al. 2006, p. 264.

2.6   Mexican situation 2050

According to several studies, the coffee production in Mexico will be strongly affected by the climate changes. It is concurrent said that the temperature will rise even if the exact increase is depending on the climate model which is used to predict the effects. According to the Camargo, the IPCC states that the global air temperature is supposed to increase between 1.1 °C and 6.6 °C[78]. More actual and precisely is the data which is published by Nelson, which states that the temperature in the Caribbean, which is on the same heights like the Sierra Madre de Chiapas, will increase between 1.67 °C and 2.66 °C till the year 2050[79]. The most geographical precisely data comes from Schroth et al., which predicts that the overall temperature increase in the Sierra Madre de Chiapas will increase between 2.1 °C and 2.2 °C by 2050 and the annual rainfall is predicted to increase by approximately 80 to 85 mm, or 4 to 5 percent at all three altitudinal ranges[80]. These information are also backed by Läderach, who predicts the changes in crop suitability, temperature and precipitation in Mesoamerica by 2050 as can be seen below.

Change in crop suitability. Red indicates how the majority of each country's coffee yield will be impacted				Contrib. to GDP (%)	Country	Colors indicate how the majority of each country's coffee-growing areas will be impacted					
						% with likely temperature change in the range of...		% with likely precipitation change in the range of...			
-40% or more	-40% to -20%	-20% to 0%	>0%			2.0-2.25 °C	2.25-2.5 °C	> -10%	-5% to -10%	-5% to 0%	0% to 5%
55.4	40.5	2.7	1.4	1.3	Costa Rica	100.0	.	.	.	100.0	.
45.5	43.7	10.9	.	2.5	El Salvador	78.3	21.7	.	1.1	98.9	.
12.9	25.5	54.2	7.4	4.2	Guatemala	60.8	39.2	.	17.4	82.6	.
38.2	49.8	11.0	1.0	8.2	Honduras	5.4	94.6	5.8	94.2	.	.
18.2	34.6	46.9	0.3	5.0	Mexico	20.6	79.4	.	49.0	50.5	0.4
35.3	32.1	32.5	0.1	7.2	Nicaragua	7.9	92.1	1.2	98.0	0.8	.

Figure 9: Projected changes in in crop suitability, temperature, and precipitation in Mesoamerica by 2050[81]

The change in the suitability is connected to the shift of the growing zones to higher altitudes. As the optimal coffee-growing elevation of *C. arabica* is currently at 1200 masl, by an increase of approximately 2°C the optimal coffee-growing elevation will shift by 400 meters to approximately 1600 masl. This shift

---

[78] Camargo, Marcelo Bento Paes de 2010, p. 239.
[79] Nelson et al. 2010, p. 94.
[80] Schroth et al. 2009, pp. 613–614.
[81] Läderach et al. 2013, p. 2.

is predicted by several studies. Also the predicted altitudinal shift can be seen in the following figure. [82,83,84]

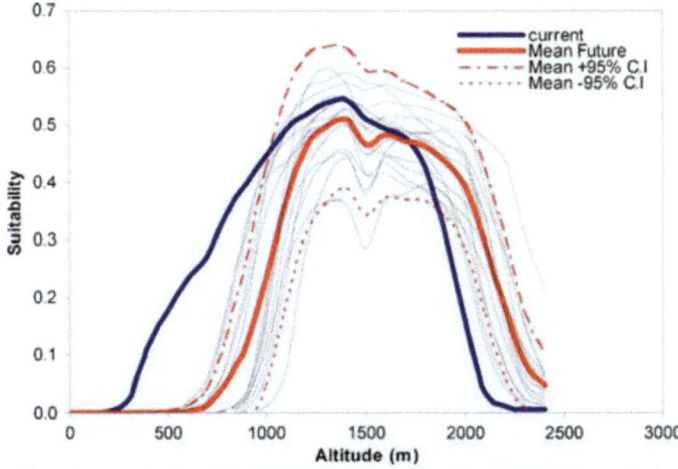

Figure 10: Altitudinal shift in suitability for Arabica coffee in the Sierra Madre de Chiapas, Mexico,[85]

The current growing zones with a suitability between 60 % and 100 % are expected to decrease from actual 265,400 ha to 6,000 ha, which means a loss of 259,400 ha, respectively about 97 %. The zone with a suitability between 40 % and 60 % will decrease by 40 % from currently 524,600 ha to 314,000 ha and the zones with a suitability under 40 % will increase from currently 1.57 million ha to 2.04 million ha. The effects can also be seen in the following figures 11, 12 and 13. [86, 87]

[82] Läderach et al. 2013, p. 2.
[83] Mayer 2013, p. 786.
[84] Vermeulen et al. 2013, p. 5.
[85] Schroth et al. 2009, p. 614.
[86] Läderach et al. 2013, p. 2.
[87] Schroth et al. 2009, pp. 613–614.

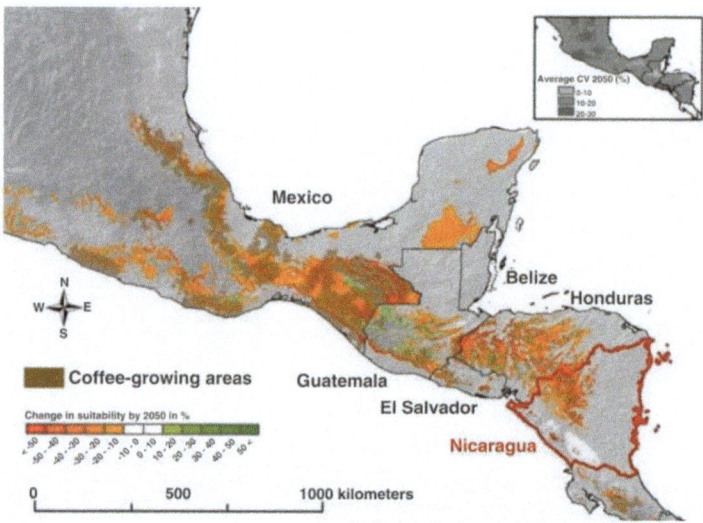

Figure 11: Projected changes in suitability in Mesoamerica by 2050 and coefficient of variance of 18 different Global Circulation Models (GCM) used for the analysis (small map).[88]

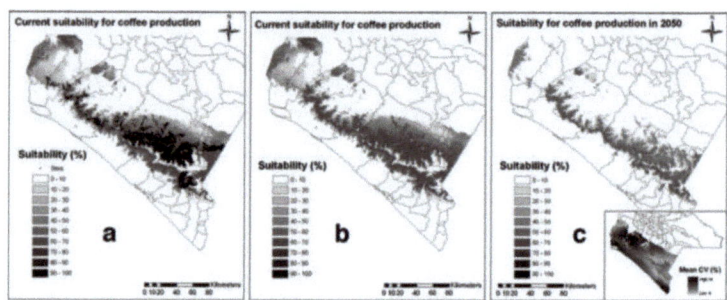

Figure 12: Current and projected climate conditions for the Sierra Madre for the period 2040 to 2069 ("2050s")[89]

---

[88] Läderach et al. 2013, p. 2
[89] Schroth et al. 2009, p. 610.

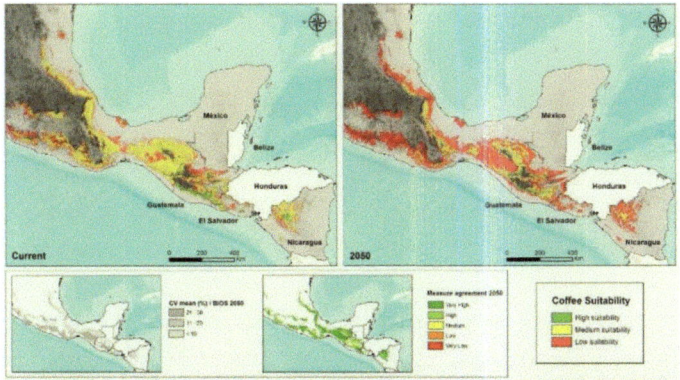

Figure 13: Prediction of the relative climatic suitability for Arabica coffee production in Mexico, Guatemala, El Salvador and Nicaragua in 2010 and 2050 (large maps), coefficient of variation (CV; small map to the left), and consistency between models (small map)[90]

Moreover it needs to be mentioned that these numbers still can't point out the true impact as the farmers cannot just move up the hills as large forested areas are protected biosphere reserves[91].

Summarised it can be said that Mexico and especially the Sierra Madre may cease to be an origin of speciality coffee and that the crop will tend to move South and uphill regions.

---

[90] Baca et al. 2014, p. 4
[91] Schroth et al. 2009

2.7   Climate change related coffee suitability changes until 2050

The study „A bitter cup: climate change profile of global production of Arabica and Robusta coffee", which was published online on the 13th December 2014 and authored by Bunn, Läderach, Ovalle-Rivera and Kirschke seeks to project current and future climate suitability for coffee production (*C. arabica* and *C. canephora*) on a global scale. For the climate variables the team used 5 different GCM's by the IPCC, as well as the WorldClim global climate data set (a set of global climate layers/ climate grids) which provides interpolated climate layers for 19 bioclimatic variables based on historical data. The information were downscaled and combined with current coffee suitability data. These data was a combination of a global database of 62,000 geo-referenced individual farms by the CIAT (Centro Internacional de Agricultura Tropical) and additional data of Brasil provided by the IBGE (Instituto Brasiliero de Geografia e Estatística). [92]

For this purpose the team developed a method which is based on several feasible parameter combinations to capture more relevant information than with just a single model to strengthen the outcome of the study. The intermediate result gave global maps of *C. arabica* and *C. canephora* that indicate suitability scores major coffee producing regions. The underlying models were applied to the outputs of the five GCM's for the RCP 2.6, RCP 6.0 and RCP 8.5 emission scenarios (Representative Concentration Pathways for greenhouse gases). The emissions scenarios where averaged to produce maps and they analysed the change in suitability score. [93]The map on the next page points out the actual major coffee regions of *C. arabica* and *C. canephora*.

---

[92] Bunn et al. 2014b, pp. 91–92
[93] Bunn et al. 2014b, p. 99

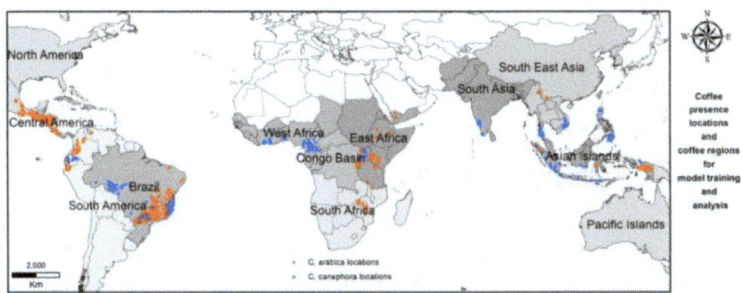

Figure 14: Global coffee location database and major coffee growing regions. Blue points represent *C. canephora* occurrence locations; orange points locations of *C. arabica* based production. Grey shading and bold names represent regions of coffee production[94]

The team calculated the difference between current and future (2050) mean suitability scores for the three RCP's and mapped them separately. The Map of the RCP 6.0 scenario, which can be seen on the next page (Figure 15), exemplifies the changes in suitability for the major coffee growing regions in the World, which is commented as follows: "The Brazilian production regions lose suitability with possible positive changes at its southern margin. In the rest of Latin America, higher altitudes become more suitable than at present. In East Africa there are positive changes in suitability in the Ethiopian, Ugandan and Kenyan highlands. In Indonesia and the Philippines there are patterns of altitudinal migration similar to South America." [95] The maps for the RCP 2.6 and RCP 8.5 emission scenarios can be found in the appendix 1 and 2.

---

[94] Bunn et al. 2014b, p. 92
[95] Bunn et al. 2014b, p. 95

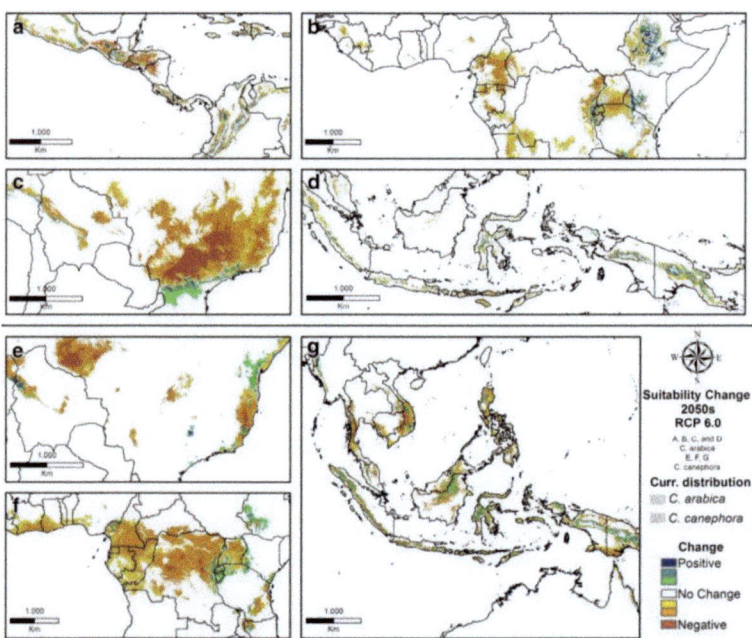

Figure 15: Suitability changes by the 2050s in the RCP 6.0 scenario; A-D: Arabica, E-G: Robusta. Hatching indicates the current suitability distribution; Warm colours represent areas with negative climate change impacts and cold colours positive changes[96]

The charts below are presenting the meridians for current climate conditions as well as the GCM outputs for all three scenarios and the distribution of suitability changes by latitude, altitude and coffee regions. The suitability score is defined by how likely a location is climatically suitable for coffee production and a higher sum of scores means that the suitable area is larger. Figure 16a shows the sum of suitability scores across latitudinal meridians and it points out that *C. arabica* would lose suitability across all latitudes besides small positive impacts around 27 °S. Figure 16b displays the suitability distribution by altitude and indicates that both species, *C. arabica* and *C. canephora* will lose large shares of total suitability whereat the largest impact will strike below 1000 masl. Figure 16c displays the sum of suitability scores for major coffee regions for current

---

[96] Bunn et al. 2014b, p. 96

conditions and means for the RCP scenario by 2050. It indicates that the largest impacts for *C. arabica* will be in Brazil, South Africa and the Congo Basin whilst the least impacted regions for *C. arabica* are East Africa and the Pacific Island region. According to the RCP 6.0 scenario the globally losses are projected to be 49 % of overall suitability score. [97]

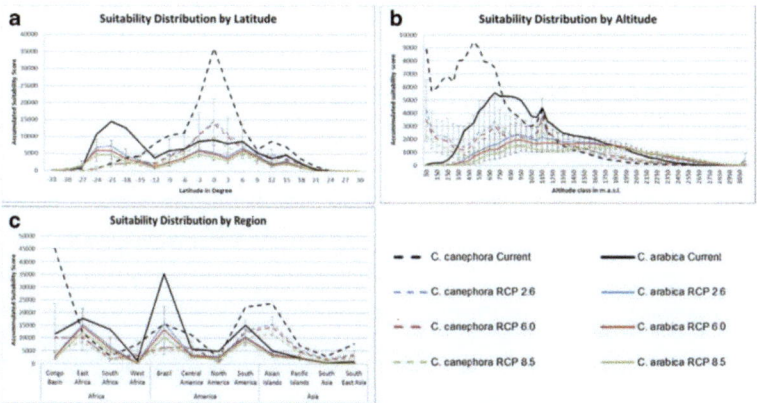

Figure 16: Distribution of suitability changes by a latitude, b altitude, c coffee regions; Continuous lines represent *C. arabica*, dashed lines *C. canephora*, black lines the current distribution, colored lines future distribution; the error bars indicate the minimum and maximum across RCP 6.0 model means[98]

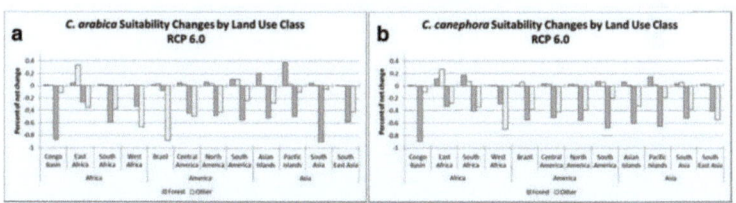

Figure 17: Distribution of suitability changes by region and the land use classes with forest cover and without forest cover by 2050 under RCP 6.0; a *C. arabica* b *C. canephora*[99]

Figure 17 distributes the suitability changes according to regions and land-use classes in the coffee producing regions by 2050 under RCP 6.0. Figure 17a,

---

[97] Bunn et al. 2014b, pp. 96–98
[98] Bunn et al. 2014b, p. 97
[99] Bunn et al. 2014b, p. 98

which represents the *C. arabica,* shows that the losses and gains in suitability are nearly equal referred to forested and non-forested areas. The largest losses in percentage share are in the Congo Basin, Brazil and South Asia whilst the substantial gains are expected in East Africa and on the Pacific Islands. [100]

Summarised it can be said that losses in suitability will more likely affect the low altitudes while higher altitudes will gain in suitability and the altitudinal migration of coffee production presumably will become a global trend. However, the dimension of the effect is depending on the local conditions and the specific impact of the climate change. A major part of the highly productive areas in Brazil and Vietnam could become unsuitable for coffee production in the future and the areas where coffee production remains feasible must adapt to the changing conditions as well as the local production systems. But not only the local systems have to adapt to the changes, also the world markets and the policy-makers need to be aware and prepared to the challenges that will occur. [101]

[100] Bunn et al. 2014b, pp. 96–98
[101] Bunn et al. 2014b, pp. 98–100

3   Methodology

3.1   Scope of the study and methods for Data Collection

To calculate the coffee balance (supply and demand) of *C. arabica* for the year 2050 in order to provide a reasonable foundation for the derivation of procurement strategy alternatives for German coffee producers, this research refers to secondary literature data. To determine the coffee balance this research relies on a two sided approach. Firstly, it calculates the climate change related changes on the global *C. arabica* production. Secondly, it uses the available data to calculate an estimated *C. arabica* demand. None of the data has been gathered by the author, all data has been taken from secondary literature like reports of the ICO, the USDA, the ECF and the IPCC, out of studies which are based on these sources or derived from those data. The used methods where simple linear regressions and extrapolations due to average annual growth rates.

3.2   Methods for calculating the coffee balance

3.2.1   How the supply of *C. arabica* for 2050 is calculated

Basis for the calculation of the supply of *C. arabica* for 2050 are the amounts of 60-kg bags which were produced in the main *C. arabica* producing countries in December 2014/15, provided by the USDA[102]. This countries are dedicated to the different producing areas which are, according to Bunn, affected differently by the climate change[103]. Given the amounts of 60-kg bags per countrythey have to be converted to kg per country for following calculations.

$$(1) \quad Produced\ coffee\ in\ kg\ (country) =$$
$$Produced\ coffee\ in\ thousand\ 60 - kg\ bags\ (country) * 60\ kg * 1000$$

For further calculations the amount of produced *C. arabica* coffee in kg per country needs to be converted into ha per country by dividing the amount of

---

[102] United States Department of Agriculture (USDA) 2014a, p. 1
[103] Bunn et al. 2014b, p. 6

produced *C. arabica* coffee in kg per country by the specific mean yield per ha of the countries, provided by the FAO[104].

$$(2) \quad Crop\ area\ per\ country\ in\ ha = \frac{Produced\ coffee\ in\ kg\ (country)}{Average\ yield\ in\ \frac{kg}{ha}}$$

The next step is to calculate the average mean suitability by region in percent of current suitability of the three major climate scenarios RCP 2.6, RCP 6.0 and RCP 8.5 in 2050, provided by Bunn[105].

$$(3) \quad Average\ mean\ suitability\ by\ region\ in\ \%\ of\ current\ suitability =$$
$$\frac{Mean\ suitabilities\ by\ region\ in\ \%\ of\ current\ suitability\ of\ RCP\ 2.6,\ RCP\ 6.0\ and\ RCP\ 8.5}{n^{RCP's}}$$

Given the average mean suitability by region in % of current suitability and the crop area per country in ha, the suitable crop area in ha per country for 2050 can be calculated as follows:

$$(4) \quad Suitable\ crop\ area\ in\ ha\ (country)\ for\ 2050 =$$
$$Crop\ area\ in\ ha\ (country) *$$
$$Average\ mean\ suitability\ by\ region\ in\ \%\ of\ current\ suitability$$

To calculate the estimated amount of *C. arabica* coffee in kg per country the formula is:

$$(5) \quad Estimated\ amount\ of\ C.arabica\ coffee\ in\ kg\ (country) =$$
$$Suitable\ crop\ arey\ in\ ha\ (country)\ for\ 2050 * Average\ yield\ in\ \frac{kg}{ha}$$

---

[104] Food and Agriculture Organization of the United States (FAO) 2015, p. 1
[105] Bunn et al. 2014b, p. 6

The formula to calculate the estimated amount of thousand 60-kg bags per country is:

$$(6) \quad Estimated\ amount\ of\ thousand\ 60 - kg\ bags\ (country) =$$

$$\frac{Estimated\ amount\ of\ C.arabica\ coffee\ in\ kg\ (country)}{\frac{60\ kg}{1000}}$$

3.2.2 How the demand of *C. arabica* for 2050 is calculated

The calculation of the demand of *C. arabica* for 2050 is divided in four parts:

- The calculation of the coffee demand for the traditional importing countries in 2050
- The calculation of the coffee demand for the emerging countries in 2050
- The calculation of the coffee demand for the exporting countries in 2050
- The calculation of the overall *C. arabica* demand in 2050

Calculation of the coffee demand for the traditional importing countries in 2050

Basis of this calculation are the numbers of total coffee demand in 2012 in thousand 60-kg bags per country, provided by the ICO[106]. To estimate the demands of the countries in 2020/2030/2040/2050 (t2), the demands of 2012 (t1) are extrapolated with an average annual growth rate of 0.5 %.

$$(7) \quad Calculated\ coffee\ consumption\ in\ t2\ in\ thousand\ 60 -$$
$$kg\ bags\ (country) = coffee\ consumption\ in\ t1\ in\ thousand\ 60 -$$
$$kg\ bags\ (country) * (1 + AAGR)^{(t2-t1)}$$

To get the total coffee demands for traditional importing countries for 2020/2030/2040/2050 (t2), the calculated coffee demand in thousand 60-kg bags per country are summarized.

---

[106] International Coffee Organisation (ICO) 2014, p. 29

(8) *Total coffee demand for traditional importing countries in t2 in thousand 60 −*
    kg bags (x1) = ∑ Calculated coffee demand in t2 in thousand 60 −
    kg bags (country)

Calculation of the coffee demand for the emerging countries in 2050

Basis of the calculation of the coffee demand of the emerging countries in 2050 are the coffee demand of China in 2012, the coffee demand of Brazil and India in 2012, the coffee demand in Russia in 2011 and the coffee demand in South Africa[107, 108, 109, 110]. The coffee demand of China for the period 2012 (t1) to 2020 (t2) is calculated with an AAGR of 12.8 %[111]. The coffee demand in China for the period 2020 (t1) to 2030/2040/2050 (t2) and the coffee demand for Brazil, India, Russia and South Africa for period 2011/2012 (t1) to 2020/2030/2040/2050 (t2) are calculated with an AAGR of 4.7 %[112]. The formula for the calculation is:

(9) *Calculated coffee demand in t2 in thousand 60 − kg bags (country) =*
    coffee demand in t1 in thousand 60 − kg bags (country) ∗
    $$(1 + AAGR)^{(t2-t1)}$$

To get the total coffee demand for emerging countries for 2020/2030/2040/2050 (t2), the calculated coffee demands in thousand 60-kg bags per country are summarized.

(10) *Total coffee demand for emerging countries in t2 in thousand kg bags (x2) =*
    ∑ Calculated coffee demand in t2 in thousand 60 − kg bags (country)

[107] International Coffee Organisation (ICO) 2011b, p. 1
[108] International Coffee Organisation (ICO) 2011c, p. 1
[109] International Coffee Organisation (ICO) 2013b, p. 10
[110] International Coffee Organisation (ICO) 2015b, p. 1
[111] International Coffee Organisation (ICO) 2013b, p. 10
[112] International Coffee Organisation (ICO) 2014, p. 13

Calculation of the coffee demand for the exporting countries in 2050

Basis for the calculation of the coffee demand for the exporting countries in 2050 are data of domestic consumption in all exporting countries which contain the years 1990 to 2012, provided by the ICO[113, 114, 115]. The quantity of complete data sets is n=47. For each country, the simple linear regression of period 1990 (t1) to 2012 is calculated. The coffee demand for the exporting countries is calculated for 2020/2030/2040/2050 (t2), with this formula:

(11) $Calculated\ coffee\ demand\ in\ t2\ in\ thousand\ 60 - kg\ bags\ (country_n) =$
$$m_n * \left((t2 - t1) + 1\right) + n_n$$

This is the formula to summarize the demand of the exporting countries:

(12) $Total\ coffee\ demand\ for\ exporting\ countries\ in\ t2\ in\ thousand\ 60 - kg\ bags\ (x3) = \sum Calculated\ coffee\ demand\ in\ t2\ in\ thousand\ 60 - kg\ bags\ (country)$

Calculation of the overall *C. arabica* demand in 2050

Baseline for the calculation of the overall coffee demand in 2020/2030/2040/2050 (t2) are the total coffee demands of the traditional importing (x1), the emerging (x2) and the exporting (x3) countries.

(13) $Overall\ coffee\ demand\ in\ t2\ in\ thousand\ 60 - kg\ bags = x1 + x2 + x3$

The next step is to calculate the development of the *C. arabica* / *C. canephora* shift until 2050 (t2). It is calculated with the data from the ICO which illustrates the *C. arabica* and *C. canephora* amounts from period 2011 (t1.1) to 2014 (t1.4) [116]. This formulas calculates the estimated share of *C. arabica* in 2050:

---

[113] International Coffee Organisation (ICO) 2001, p. 1
[114] International Coffee Organisation (ICO) 2011a, p. 1
[115] International Coffee Organisation (ICO) 2015b, p. 1
[116] International Coffee Organisation (ICO) 2015a, p. 1

$$(14) \; C.\,arabica \; share \; in \; year \; (t) =$$

$$\frac{C.arabica \; amount \; of \; year \; (t)}{C.arabica \; amount \; of \; year \; (t) + C.canephora \; amount \; of \; year \; (t)}$$

The next step is calculating the simple linear regression. It is used in combination of t1.1 (2011) and t2 (2050) to calculate the *C. arabica* share in 2050.

$$(15) \; Calculated \; C.\,arabica \; share \; in \; t2 = m_n * \big((t2 - t1.1) + 1\big) + n_n$$

The last step is to calculate the estimated *C. arabica* demand in t2 (2050) in thousand 60-kg bags by adapting the calculated *C. arabica* share in t2 (2050) to the overall coffee demand in t2 (2050) in thousand 60-kg bags.

$$(16) \; Estimated \; C.\,arabica \; demand \; in \; t2 \; in \; thousand \; 60 - kg \; bags = \\ C.\,arabica \; share \; in \; t2 * Overall \; coffee \; demand \; in \; t2 \; in \; thousand \; 60 - \\ kg \; bags$$

4   Results

4.1   Coffee Balance 2050

4.1.1   Results

The suitable production area of *C. arabica* of all countries studies amounts to 3,521,144.57 ha in 2050 compared to 6,622,143.91 ha in 2013. This equates to a loss of 46.83 % of the suitable area for *C. arabica*. The amount of thousand 60-kg bags decreases from 88.743 in 2014 to 43.966 in 2050, which represents a loss of 50.46 % of the world's *C. arabica* yields. The figures 18 and 19 demonstrate the changes regarding to the suitable production areas and the expected yield. For more detailed information please see appendix 3.

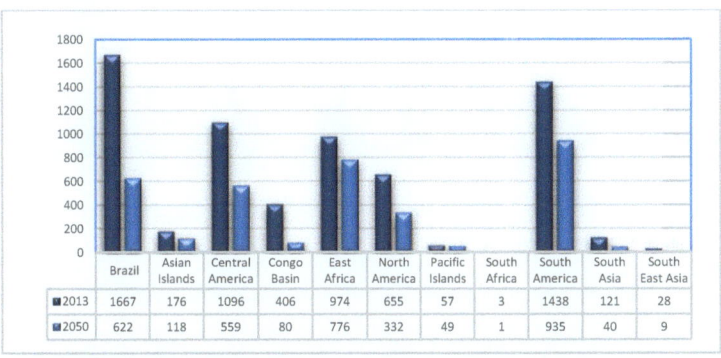

	Brazil	Asian Islands	Central America	Congo Basin	East Africa	North America	Pacific Islands	South Africa	South America	South Asia	South East Asia
▪2013	1667	176	1096	406	974	655	57	3	1438	121	28
▪2050	622	118	559	80	776	332	49	1	935	40	9

Figure 18: Suitable production areas for *C. arabica* in thousand ha (2013 to 2050)

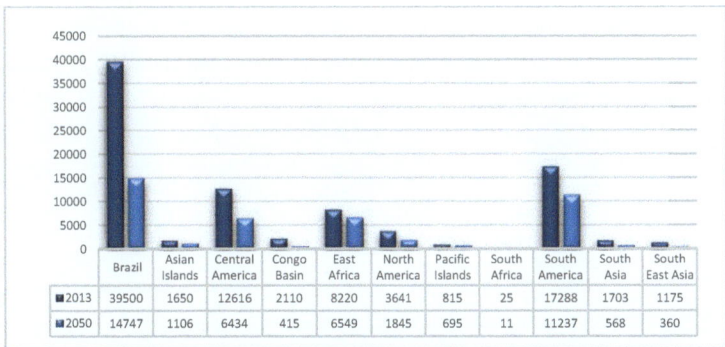

	Brazil	Asian Islands	Central America	Congo Basin	East Africa	North America	Pacific Islands	South Africa	South America	South Asia	South East Asia
▪2013	39500	1650	12616	2110	8220	3641	815	25	17288	1703	1175
▪2050	14747	1106	6434	415	6549	1845	695	11	11237	568	360

Figure 19: *C. arabica* yield for production areas in thousand 60-kg bags (2013 to 2050

The expected demand of coffee by 2050 is more than twice of the actual amount of coffee demand. As the actual demand (2012) is at 145.274 thousand 60-kg bags (*C. arabica* and *C. canephora*), the demand for 2050 is at 319.088 thousand 60-kg bags (*C. arabica* and *C. canephora*), as shown in figure 20. For more detailed information please see appendix 4.

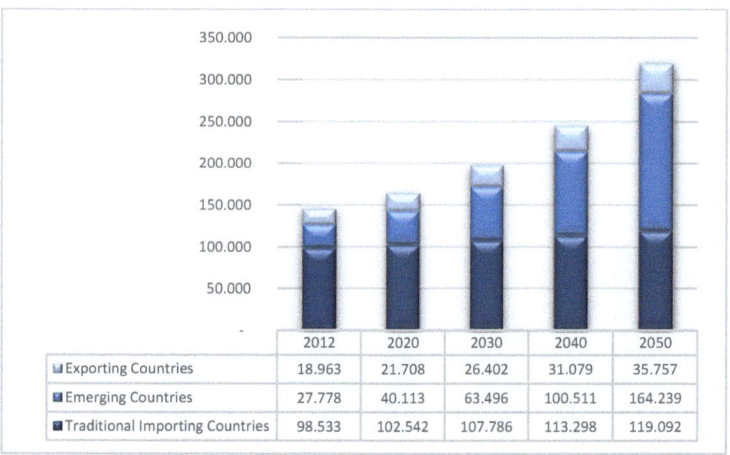

	2012	2020	2030	2040	2050
▣ Exporting Countries	18.963	21.708	26.402	31.079	35.757
▣ Emerging Countries	27.778	40.113	63.496	100.511	164.239
▣ Traditional Importing Countries	98.533	102.542	107.786	113.298	119.092

Figure 20: Projected coffee demand in thousand 60-kg bags (2012 to 2050)

The demand of the traditional importing countries and the exporting countries will rise at a smaller percentage while the demand in the emerging countries will more than sextuple within the 38 years from 2012 to 2050, if the demand keeps growing like in the past years. Figure 21 demonstrates the changing demands for the emerging countries.

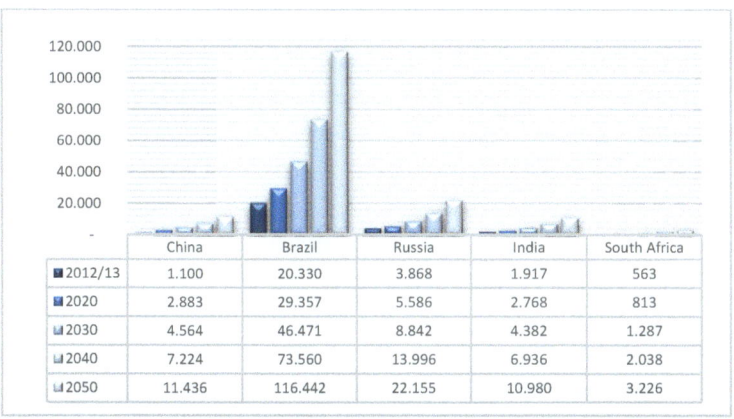

	China	Brazil	Russia	India	South Africa
■ 2012/13	1.100	20.330	3.868	1.917	563
■ 2020	2.883	29.357	5.586	2.768	813
◫ 2030	4.564	46.471	8.842	4.382	1.287
◫ 2040	7.224	73.560	13.996	6.936	2.038
◫ 2050	11.436	116.442	22.155	10.980	3.226

Figure 21: Projected demand changes of the emerging countries (2012 to 2050)

The *C. arabica/C. canephora* ratio in the demand will slightly shift towards *C. canephora*. In 2050 the percentage of *C. canephora* will be 47.02 %, which leaves a ratio of 52.98 % for *C. arabica*. This leads to a calculated demand of 169.053 thousand 60-kg bags of *C. arabica* in 2050.

4.1.2   Analysis

The objective of this thesis is to derivate procurement strategy alternatives of german coffee producers due to climate related changes on the global green coffee market and the calculations clearly show that the adaption of the strategies is needed as the demand of *C. arabica* cannot even roughly be satisfied in 2050. Considering the results only 26.01 % of the *C. arabica* demand worldwide could be satisfied. This is based on a few crucial factors.

The first major factor that leads to this loss of *C. arabica* is the increasing mean temperature in the main production areas of *C. arabica* which lowers the suitability of the coffee plantation to a point, where the cultivation is economically unprofitable. At the time of writing this study the data provided by the Bunn indicated an average area loss of 48.39 % in the growing areas, but aligned to the countries just 44.89 % of the land will not be suitable in 2050. However, both indicators show a large change.

The second major factor is the raising demand of coffee. As stated in 2.2, the actual rates of growth for emerging countries are increasing as the populations of the countries are getting larger and the residents are getting wealthier. Whilst the AAGR for the emerging markets is at 4.7 %, the AAGR for China is expected to be at 12.8 %, at least for the next few years. This leads to a more than six fold increase of the demand in the emerging countries till 2050. Compared to this, the growing demand in the exporting and the traditional importing countries is marginal.

In a nutshell: The results of the calculation are confirming the assumption from the beginning and frame the foundation for the further steps of this thesis.

4.2   Procurement strategy alternatives

This research has calculated the coffee balance for 2050 to find procurement alternatives. However, the procurement alternatives have to be adapted to the climate related chances which leads to different approached to adaption planning.

As written by Vermeulen (et al.), adaption planning can incorporate scientific information from both projections of climatic impacts and assessments of adaptive capacity. Impact approaches are using statistical and mechanistic models to calculate possible outcomes under certain circumstances. The basis for this are climate projections and global circulation models, their impacts on the local climates and microclimates and therefore the crop physiology, yields as well as the following prices, quality parameters and the impact on the human welfare and nutrition. Capacity approaches are focussing on existing capacities and vulnerabilities of socio-economic groups such as communities, industries or countries.[117] Considering that this adaptions are impact-based, the contemporary necessity to realise the adaptions is given.

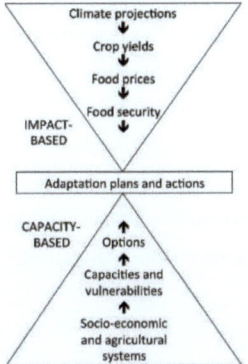

Figure 22: Impact and capacity approaches to adaption planning[118]

---

[117] Vermeulen et al. 2013, p. 8358
[118] Vermeulen et al. 2013, p. 8358

Nowadays domestic and multinational corporations are not only challenged to develop good products, but also to create new, environmentally sustainable ways of production, shipment and packaging. At the same time, the needs of the shareholder and different stakeholders like environmental organisations, world trade regulations, national and international laws and the consumers have to be considered. But not only the corporations have to change: The entire coffee supply chain must restructure itself to prepare for changes in sourcing, production and continuative adaption. [119, 120]

The supply chain is the factor which is most critical and significant for the German coffee producers, especially by the time the demand exceeds the supply. Consequentially German coffee producers should not only adapt their own strategies, they also should expand their influence and their ownership along the whole coffee supply chain to have the best initial position for negotiations and acquisitions when the imbalance of supply and demand occurs. To achieve this position, there are plenty different approaches and the best way should be a mix out of the complete range to minimize economical and financial risks. But at the approaches can be far-reaching adaptions which can cost huge amounts of time and money- like the breeding of new coffee species- it would not be reasonable for one company to approach this adaptions on her own. [121]

On the other hand and from the corporate social responsibility point of view, a strict focus on the economic needs of the German coffee producers would likely lead to negative impacts among the bottom parts of the supply chain like the farmers, the local organisations and the nature itself.

This is also backed by a study of Blitzer et al., which evaluates different sustainability partnerships and comes to following conclusion: "Partnerships in their current form are Northern based models that allow for Northern actors to

---

[119] Closs et al. 2011, p. 102
[120] Läderach et al. 2013, pp. 3–4
[121] Preibisch 2012, p. 4

be overrepresented whereas Southern actors often lack significant participation. [...] Because of their reliance on standards and the lack of coordination of efforts and strategies, they compete with each other and most of all, with Fair Trade and organic coffee on definitions of 'sustainable coffee'. [...] As a consequence, partnerships cause for more product differentiation and an increasingly broader pattern of specialty markets. In this perspective, the marketing and promotion of partnerships - embedded into anecdotes of partnership activities and keywords such as 'sustainability', 'biodiversity protection' and 'livelihood improvement' - fits into the 'boom' of differentiated coffees in coffee bars such as Starbucks that sell an ambiance and a lifestyle. [...] The increasingly differentiated coffee market seems to hold opportunities for only a limited number of coffee producers, whereas the larger part of the 25 million coffee farmers will not be reached and their continuing problems will not be solved. [...] In order for that to happen, partnerships must engage in a more honest and holistic dialog that addresses all sustainability challenges of the coffee chain and does not limit its definition of 'sustainable coffee' to certified coffee without looking at the bigger picture." [122]

Different studies have evaluated certain adaption strategies like genetic breeding, shading management systems, value chain adaption strategies, diversification, conversion of soil and water sources as well as organisation among small producers, microfinance and development aid and training and development. The sum of adaption strategies can be divided into three groups according to their main areas of influence after the basic concept of sustainability; into environmental sustainable approaches, economical sustainable approaches and social sustainable approaches, although all approaches have influences in all three areas. The following subchapters are introducing a set of potential approaches.

---

[122] Bitzer et al. 2008, pp. 281–282

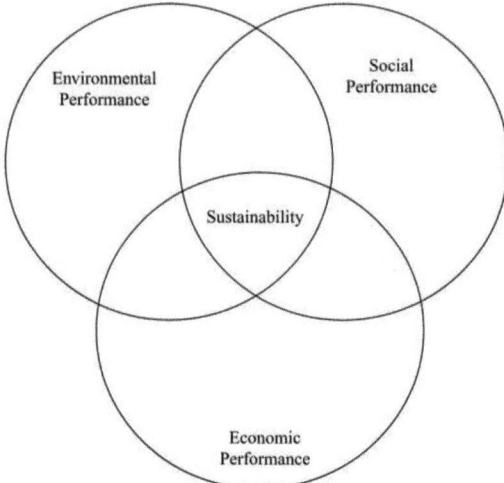

Figure 23: Sustainability: the triple bottom line[123]

[123] Carter, Rogers 2008, p. 365

4.2.1   Environmental sustainable approaches

Even though the contribution to environmental matters in the coffee production are by far bigger compared to other producing industries, many challenges are remaining and some large challenges are going to come which require special attention. The exemplary approaches are shade management, preventing soil erosion and water efficiency.

Shade management

Shade management, also known as arborisation, is a way to control the microclimate within a coffee plantation with the help of trees. There are several trees which are suitable for shading such as cedrinho, macadamia, banana prate, avocado and dwarfish coconut whose roots also reduce the physical damage of tropical storms causing floods and landslides. [124, 125] Besides that some of them are also offering a chance for a secondary income - shading management - as every system - has its advantages and disadvantages.

The main advantage is that shading can compensate temperature fluctuations and lower the mean temperature which can lead to an increased suitability for *C. arabica* plants. This allows coffee to be grown where non-shaded plantations are not efficient anymore. A study done by Lin in 2007 that deals with "Agroforestry management as an adaptive strategy against potential microclimate extremes in coffee agriculture" shows that shaded systems have the ability to soften microclimatic extremes and protect the coffee plants by keeping them closer to their ideal temperature minimum and maximum. It's also said that this study is backed up by various previous studies like Barradas and Fanjul (1986) who found that the thermal amplitude increases nearly two times when shade was removed, as well as Kirkpatrick (1953) who found that minimum temperatures where about 6.5 °C lower and the humidity variations were greater in unshaded sites. [126]

---

[124] Camargo, Marcelo Bento Paes de 2010, pp. 244–245
[125] Schroth et al. 2009, p. 620
[126] Lin 2007, p. 92

Another environmental advantage of shaded plantations is the increased diversity of birds. A study done by Greenberg et al. from 1994 shows that approximately 105 different species of birds can be found in each shaded plantation in eastern Chiapas, Mexico. The density is only exceeded regionally by the tropical forest. [127] In addition Hudson (2004) mentioned that according to the Smithsonian sun-grown plantations supports 90 % fewer species.

On the other hand shaded plantations just can hold between 1,000 and 3,000 plants per hectare, while sun-grown varieties can hold up to 10,000 plants per hectare which offers the farmers a considerable income benefit as the plants can also produce more coffee cherries due to higher photosynthetic rates.

Summarised shade management is an easy and comparatively inexpensive way to maintain a certain suitability to warming areas whilst supporting the microclimate, the soil and the local fauna.

Preventing soil erosion
For any crop, the soil the crop is growing in is one of the main factors for a successful cultivation. Hudson (2004) cited Justus von Liebig's definition of "rational agriculture" as based on a "principle of restitution; ... (on) Giving back to the fields the conditions of their own fertility" (in Foster, 2000: 153) [...][128]. Since the coffee plantations are expanding, processing is getting more centralized in plants over the time and shifted from the farms to the fringes of urban centers. This eliminates the residual products, like the pulp and the skin of the bean, to return to the plantations as a natural fertilizer. Instead the residues are processed in a different way whilst the crops are fertilized with nitrogen, potassium and calcium, which tends to be exhausted by the coffee plants. Not only can the dissipation of natural fertilizer be minimized by using the residual products, also potential water pollution through an excessive use of chemical fertilizers can be prevented.[129]

---

[127] Greenberg et al. 1997, p. 501
[128] Hudson, Hudson 2004, p. 139
[129] International Coffee Organisation (ICO) 2014, pp. 20–21

Another way to prevent soil erosion is to maintain a vegetated soil through the rainy seasons with weed. Not only that the grass roots prevent the top soil from being flushed away, they also slightly loose up the soil so the soil water retention capacity increases and the stored water helps to increase the organic matter tenor. Another positive factor is the reduced soil and air temperatures, which allowed to establish coffee plants in Brazilian marginal areas of low altitude where the mean air temperatures were too high for the usual cultivation of *C. arabica*. [130]

Another interesting parameter of the soil is the distribution of mycorrhizal fungal spores in the soil. As observed by Cardoso (et al.), the distribution of mycorrhizal fungal spores is completely different in soils under agroforestry and monoculture coffee systems. The relation between the root dry weight and the number of spores of AFM (arbuscular mycorrhizal fungi) differs in the concentration as well as in the depth where the spores can be found, as they can be found in a lower depth under agroforestry. This leads to the fact that a greater mycorrhizal activity in deeper soil layers may be important to make more potassium available to the plant, as the potassium in a deeper layer is in a more available form for the plants. To achieve this, a combination between coffee plants and trees is recommended. [131]

Water efficiency

Coffee is not only being harvested, also a major part of the coffee is further processed near the plantation. The coffee that is processed by wet method is called washed or parchment coffee. During this process the fruit pulp and the thin skin which covers the bean are removed by a pulper. The pulper is a machine that comes in different types (drum pulper, disc pulper, vertical spiral drum pulper) but every machine needs an adequate amount of fresh water. Another process that needs water is an additional process to the fermentation: The mechanical removal of mucilage. The fermentation is a process where the

[130] Camargo, Marcelo Bento Paes de 2010, pp. 244–245
[131] Cardoso et al. 2003, pp. 40–42

mucilage layer on the parchment is broken down into non-sticky substances. The mechanical way uses partially/completely fermented beans which are soaked in fresh water for 12 hours and after this time the beans are further processed. This step is used to improve visual appearance and quality by removing substances which impart hardness to brew. [132]

A study done by Haddis and Devîn (2007) evaluated the "Effect of effluent generated from coffee processing plant on the water bodies and human health in its vicinity" in Zimma zone (Ethiopia). Water bodies were tested near to a coffee processing plant and they came to the result that the coffee processing wastewaters (CPWW) are heavily polluted with organic load, nutrients and suspended matter. For example the values of temperature, pH, BOD, COD, suspended soils phosphate and nitrate of the water before entering of the CPWW were 15 °C, 6.5, 120 mg/l, 176 mg/l 520 mg/l, 2.3 mg/l and 4.0 mg/l. The values of the parameters after the entering of the CPWW were 18 °C, 5.15, 7800 mg/l, 9780 mg/l, 2880 mg/l, 4.10 mg/l and 7.5 mg/l, so all parameters (except the temperature) were much more than the prescribed limits by the WHO. And as this CPWW is flowing directly into the water bodies which are used by the people residing near to the plant and were utilizing the water for domestic purposes, they were suffering from serve health problems like spinning sensations, eye irritations and breathing problems. [133]

Additional to this pollutions there can be pollution caused by excessive use of chemical fertilizers, pesticides and herbicides due to not properly skilled farmers who do not know the exact effects of the used chemicals and how to use them in a health-oriented way. [134]

An experiment done by Selvamurugan (at al.) in India is tackling the CPWW problem using an upflow anaerobic hybrid reactor (UAHR) which was developed by Lettinga. The outcome of the experiment is that the CPWW is

[132] Murthy, Madhava Naidu 2012, pp. 47–48
[133] Haddis, Devi 2008, p. 261
[134] International Coffee Organisation (ICO) 2014, pp. 20–21

suitable for biological treatment and under certain circumstances the continuous aeration of wastewater resulted in maximum reduction of BOD (74.6 %), COD (68.6 %) and total solids (49.3 %) whilst producing methane. This approach followed by aeration and constructed wetland technology is well suited to be an eco-friendly approach for CPWW treatment. [135], [136], [137]

4.2.2   Economical sustainable approaches

Economical sustainable approaches are mainly focused on the monetary, value increasing and pricey factors. The environmental factors are subordinated. Also it has to be considered, that this approaches have the goals to be economical sustainable for German coffee producers and not for every element in the supply chain. Main approaches are the breeding of new species as the programs are pricey and coffee politics and influences.

Breeding

According to Hein et al. (2006) there are three main reasons for breeding coffee. First reason is to breed pest and disease resistant varieties. The three major pests and diseases that hamper the worldwide coffee production are the coffee berries disease (CBD), Meliodogyne spp. and coffee rust. CBD is a fungus that can destroy the whole yield of a plantation without harming the plants themselves. Meliodogyne is a root-knot nematode that attacks and destroys the roots of coffee, tobacco, cotton and other plants. Coffee rust, which is caused by the fungus Hemileia vastatrix, is the most important coffee disease worldwide. The costs of damage by this three diseases were over 2 billion US dollar in 2014. [138] For more detailed information see appendix 5.

---

[135] Selvamurugan et al. 2010, p. 1686
[136] Selvamurugan et al. 2010, p. 1686
[137] Selvamurugan et al. 2010, p. 1690
[138] Hein, Gatzweiler 2006, p. 179

The second reason for breeding is to develop low caffeine coffee cultivar. These varieties are developed to avoid costs for decaffeinating as the consumption of decaffeinated coffee is increasing, especially in Eastern Europe. [139]

The third reason is to develop varieties with increased yields. Within the last 20 years the average annual growth rate of coffee yields was around 1.7 %. This was not only achieved by other coffee varieties, but they had a high contribution. But coffee hybrids have not only an increased yield, they also have a greater yield stability over location and time, as it is cited by Bertrand (et al., 1997). [140]

The Instituto Agronômico Campinas (IAC) is one of the leading institutions when it comes to genetic coffee breeding. The cultivars developed several coffee varieties like Bourbon, Icatu, Acaiá and Obatã. The developed breeds represent more than 90 % of the *C. arabica* trees cultivated in Brazil. Some of the varieties are resistant's against diseases like coffee rust, have a more compact size and/or are especially good in yield and quality. These varieties have increased the yield in Brazil significantly, whilst cultivated even on marginal lands with unfavourable air temperature. [141]

Furthermore there are more possible approaches for effective breeding instead of simply hybridizing the different varieties. A research group in Brazil opened a new window as they succeeded in mapping of the *C. arabica* genome. The result is a useful database with over 200,000 expressed sequence tags which can help to breed, facilitate and cultivate varieties with outstanding performances under adverse environmental conditions. [142]

According to Hein et al., it is assumed that breeding programs would require approximately 15 years for breeding. Therefore the new varieties could be cultivated from year 16 onwards and as the first yield appears after three to four

---

[139] Hein, Gatzweiler 2006, p. 178
[140] Hein, Gatzweiler 2006, p. 179
[141] Camargo, Marcelo Bento Paes de 2010, p. 245
[142] DaMatta, Ramalho, José D. Cochicho, p. 75

years, first benefits will occur approximately 20 years after starting the breeding program. Although the value of new species cannot be calculated preliminary, because it is not possible to identify all potential benefits of the new species, the value of it can be higher than expected. [143]

The costs of a breeding program are rarely discussed but Hein et al. mentioned an ongoing Regional Coffee Wilt Programme (RCWP) whose goal it is to reduce damages by Coffee Wilt (tracheomycosis) in African coffee plants[144].

The report "A synthesis of the work of the Regional Coffee Wilt Programme 2000–2007" by the CABI (Commonwealth Agricultural Bureaux International) published in 2009, who supervised this project, rises the complete costs for this project to € 720,000, £ 110,059 and US$ 8,591,587. The project took seven years, no new species where breed just a slightly changed one and the major part of the project was to teach farmers on how to identify and treat the disease. In total they trained 1,000,836 farmers in five different countries in Africa. [145], [146]

Summarised, breeding new species and varieties has a great potential for the coffee industry as it can help to increase yields, weaken the climatic impacts and prevent damage caused by pests and diseases. The costs for a far-reaching breeding program, as well as the development of new cultivating strategies and the training of the farmers have to be considered at a scale far above US$ 9 million. But on a long-term view breeding new species and varieties is unavoidable for maintaining the *C. arabica* production at a certain level.

---

[143] Hein, Gatzweiler 2006, p. 181
[144] Hein, Gatzweiler 2006, pp. 180–181
[145] Phiri, Baker 2009, p. 173
[146] Phiri, Baker 2009, pp. 35–36

Coffee politics and influence

Unfortunately there are not much public accessible information about this topic, nevertheless this approach needs to be considered as the worldwide situation has changed within the last decades.

Until 1989 the largest part of the global coffee supply chain was controlled by the International Coffee Agreement (ICA), which was managed by the ICO. The ICA was an international agreement which was not particularly driven by any actor, nor by a state. The international coffee trade was regulated by a commodity agreement whilst the entry barriers at farming and domestic trade were mediated by the governments. But after the ICA failed to negotiate exports quotas in 1989, the influence on the global coffee supply chain vanished. Nowadays the global coffee supply chain is mainly buyer-driven as most of the strategic choices are made by large roasters. For example roasters are setting entry barriers for countries and farmers by setting minimum levels for coffee quality and purchase quantity.[147] For more detailed information about changing characteristics of the coffee supply chain see appendices 6 and 7.

Also the institutional framework has changed as the ICA or rather the ICO have lost their influence. The market regulations is not regulated by quotas anymore. Nowadays - as there are not so many trade limits left - the prices and quantities of traded coffee are fluctuating and depending on political negotiations, supply and demand which indicates that the power is transferred from producers to consumers.[148]

But not only the farmers and the producing countries are losing influence - also companies between this two parties like international coffee traders have their struggles to keep involved in the process. They had to revise their functional roles, invest in new structures like logistic systems and had to become more

---

[147] Ponte 2002, p. 1112
[148] Ponte 2002, pp. 1112–1114

active/involved in the producing countries. The figures below show the mayor companies of coffee trading and coffee roasting and manufacturing in 1998. [149]

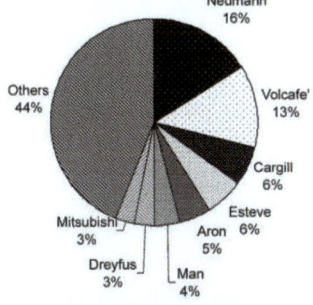

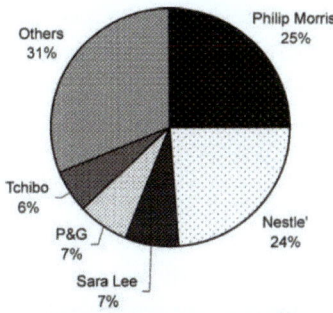

Figure 24: Green coffee market share by international trade company (1998), in percentage. Source: van Dijk et al. (1998, p. 34). [150]

Figure 25: Market share of roasting and instant manufacturing companies (1998), in percentage. Source: van Dijk et al. (1998, p. 52). [151]

Out of the listed companies just Neumann and Tchibo are German companies. Volcafe, Esteve and Nestle are from Switzerland, Dreyfus is located in the UK and Cargill, Aron, Philip Morris (meanwhile Mondelēz International), Sara Lee and P&G are based in the United States. Even though a lot of the foreign companies have production sites in Germany, the major decisions are made abroad. Shares are going to change again, as Mondelēz International is going to fusion with D.E Master Blenders 1753, a Dutch coffee company[152]. This supports the approach that German coffee producers should expand their influence and their ownership along the whole coffee supply chain.

---

[149] Ponte 2002, pp. 1115–1117
[150] Ponte 2002, p. 1108
[151] Ponte 2002, p. 1108
[152] Mondelez International 2014, p. 1

4.2.3   Social sustainable approaches

The focus of social sustainable approaches is to develop processes and structures which meet the needs of the community that is involved in the process. For example these needs can be health issues, labour rights, financial independence and community development. The main approaches are fair trade as well as financial and development aid.

Fair Trade

At first it has to be mentioned that "Fairtrade" is used by Fairtrade International to certify and identify their products. In this case I use "Fair Trade" to refer to the general initiative and movement without specifying a particular certification.

Dragusanu et al. adequate described Fair Trade as follows: "Fair Trade attempts to achieve several goals; the primary and best-known is to provide prices that deliver a basic livelihood for producers. In addition, Fair Trade has a number of other goals, including longer-term buyer–seller relationships that facilitate greater access to financing for producers; improved working conditions; the creation and/or maintenance of effective producer or worker organizations; and the use of environmentally friendly production processes. A third-party certification process regularly checks that producers and suppliers adhere to a set of requirements whose purpose is to achieve these objectives. The Fair Trade label that is displayed on certified products is a signal to consumers that the product was produced and traded in accordance with these requirements." [153]

The Fair Trade movement was developed during the era of regulated coffee trade under the ICA in the early 1960s but gained publicity in the 1990s when the Agreement collapsed[154]. The main goal of the movement is to empower producers in the global South by providing them with better conditions in pricing, long-lasting contracts and development resources whilst promoting responsible

---

[153] Dragusanu et al. 2014, p. 218
[154] Jaffee 2012, p. 105

consumption and providing consumers with socially and environmentally friendly products[155]. The first Fair Trade commodity was coffee. Nowadays also commodities like bananas, cocoa and tea are certified and traded as Fair Trade but coffee remains the most important commodity in terms of volume and sales[156].

The certification is based on a range of commandments from different stakeholders, including consumers, which are getting more and more environmentally conscious and are increasingly emphasising to know where, how and under which conditions a product is produced[157]. And as cited above, a third-party certification guarantees that the requirements are kept.

The following part describes four of the major goals of the Fair Trade movement:

- Price floor
- Stability and access to credits
- Working conditions
- Environmental protection.
-

Price Floor

One of the main principles of Fair Trade is a price that gives the farmers and workers a stable income. For this purpose Fair Trade buyers agree to pay at least the minimum price for certified goods. By guaranteeing a minimum price the financial risks that growers would face in another coffee crisis is reduced.
[158]

The levels of the minimum prices for certified commodities are set by the Fairtrade Labeling Organizations (FLO). The FLO formed when all the European licensing initiatives created an international body to homogenize the standards and administer certifications and is based in Bonn, Germany. The

---

[155] Raynolds 2012, p. 276
[156] Jaffee 2012, p. 95
[157] Jaffee 2012, p. 98
[158] Dragusanu et al. 2014, pp. 219–220

first floor prices were established in 1988 and were based on studies of production and living costs for farmer households. [159], [160] Since the floor price was established in 1988, the market price mostly was higher than the Fair Trade but as the prices crashed in the late 1990s and the early 2000s, the price floor provided the certified farmers with a certain income and reduced their financial risk. The figure below displays the coffee price development from 1989 to 2014. [161]

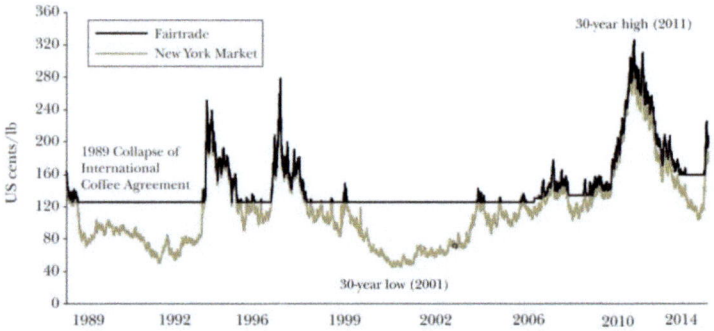

Figure 26: Comparison of Fairtrade and Market Prices for Coffee, 1989–2014[162]

Dragusanu mentions three studies who confirm the positive effects for the farmers.

The first is made by Méndez (2010). He surveyed 469 households in El Salvador, Guatemala, Mexico and Nicaragua during the coffee harvest 2003/2004 and found a significant positive relationship between average sales price for coffee and both Fair Trade and Organic certification. The second one is from Arnould, Plastina and Ball (2009) who examined 1,269 certified farmers from Nicaragua, Peru and Guatemala in 2004-2005. They came to the conclusion that the farmers not only have higher prices, they also have greater sales and higher incomes than not certified farmers. The third is from Jaffee (2009) who examined 51 coffee producers in Mexico between 2001 and 2005.

[159] Jaffee 2012, p. 103
[160] Jaffee 2012, p. 107
[161] Dragusanu et al. 2014, pp. 219–220
[162] Dragusanu et al. 2014, p. 220

His conclusion was that certified farmers are less likely to experience food shortages and that their diets contained more products like meat, milk and cheese which are more expensive. [163, 164]

Stability and access to credit

As the monetary influence is not only limited to the farmers, also the local producer cooperatives are earning more money and therefore the complete stability of the whole involved community is increasing. This further leads to an increased amount of credits, which certified farmers can get of their cooperatives. Most of the credits are pre-harvest credits as this allows them to make investments in their production and reduces their risk of financial exposure in the month before harvest. Some cooperatives also state that the sheer certification of a farm increases its credit worthiness and that access to financial services is facilitated. [165, 166]

Dragusanu states that Raynolds (2009) finds that the cooperatives view financing as the second major benefit of Fair Trade. This is also backed by Bacon et al. (2008) who descried that, out of a sample of 177 coffee farmers in Nicaragua, 77 % of their cooperative provided pre-harvest credit. [167]

Working conditions

Fair Trade certifications are not only focused on the farm, the process and the product; also the workers are in their focus. The certifications provide a set of rules which improves the conditions for the workers like workers' freedom of association, safe and equitable working conditions, the absence of forced or child labour and salaries that are at least the established minimum wage. [168]

---

[163] Dragusanu et al. 2014, p. 223
[164] Dragusanu et al. 2014, p. 224
[165] Bitzer et al. 2008, p. 277
[166] Giovannucci, Ponte 2005, p. 295
[167] Dragusanu et al. 2014, p. 228
[168] Dragusanu et al. 2014, p. 232

Additional another pillar of some Fair Trade certifications is the further education of farmers and workers. The education aims at training and developing the workforce in various ways that they can understand and transcript the meaning and importance of the sustainability movement, their regulations and their benefits, like environmental improvement. The education can be broken down into the three categories employee relations, business management practices and talent development. [169] For more information see appendix 8.

But not only the farmers and workers have access to an improved education. Gitter et al. (2012) examined the effect of participation in Fair Trade/organic certification on the education of children in coffee producing households in Southern Mexico, and finds that children from households with access to certified markets achieved more years of schooling. [170]

Environmental protection
Fair Trade labels often include environmentally friendly farming practices like shading, producing compost and applying it to the plants, building terraces and counter rows. According to Dragusanu, Jaffee (2009) compared 51 Mexican coffee farmers (26 Fair Trade, 25 conventional) and came to the conclusion that the differences in their implemented environmental farming practices are statistically significant. The figure 27 illustrates the results of the study. [171]

---

[169] Closs et al. 2011, p. 106
[170] Gitter et al. 2012, p. 460
[171] Dragusanu et al. 2014, p. 229

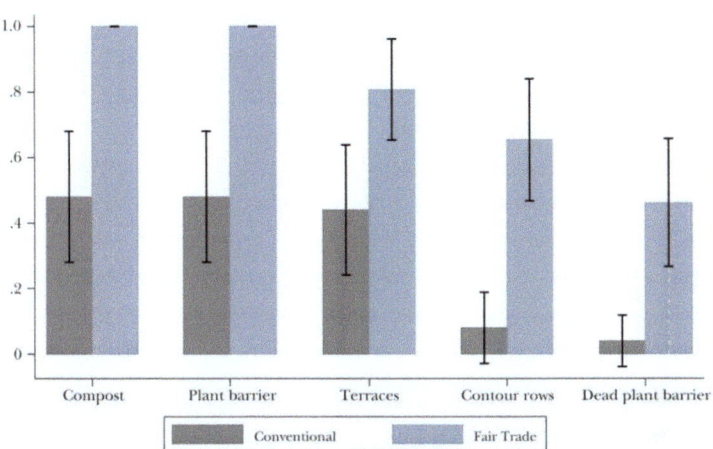

Figure 27: Differences in Environmental Practices between Fair Trade and Conventional Coffee Producers in Oaxaca, Mexico (proportion of producers engaging in environmental conservation practices)[172]

Summarized, Fair Trade - with its NGO's and the social movement - had a large impact in the social and environmental development of the coffee industry by creating alternative economic networks and this effect can be expected to carry on. It also changed the control of the coffee supply chains as when transnational corporations adopt Fair Trade labels to their product range, also parts of their activities are partial controlled by third parties. [173]

Another aspect for the continuous publicity are big coffee companies like Starbucks or Cafédirect, which are already sourcing a major part of their coffee from Fair Trade certified producers as this gives this companies the opportunity to validate their ethical commitments, their interest in social and environmental issues (Corporate Social Responsibility) as well as the requirements of their

---

[172] Dragusanu et al. 2014, p. 230
[173] Raynolds 2012, p. 286

customers. [174, 175, 176] All in all Fair Trade is a far-reaching approach whose positive impact is confirmed in social, environmental and economic matters.

Microfinance and development aid

As Haupt (2006) states: „The Federal Republic of Germany promotes the development and expansion of microfinance organizations through financial and technical cooperation." [177] Indeed German companies have several ways to improve the situation of workers, farmers and cooperatives in the producing countries to not only improve the quantity and quality of products, the working/living conditions, education and the health, but also to enable the possibility helping people help themselves.

Next to foundations like the Hanns R. Neumann Foundation (see http://www.hrnstiftung.org/) and initiatives like the Coffee & Climate Initiative (see http://www.coffeeandclimate.org/), a large number of financial investments and development aid is provided by the BMZ (Federal Ministry for Economic Cooperation and Development). The BMZ has launched the "develoPPP.de" programme in 1999, which is focused to "Develop partnerships with the private sector" and is executed by the German Development finance institute (DEG), Deutsche Gesellschaft für Internationale Zusammenarbeit GmbH (GIZ) and sequa GmbH (German non-profit development organization). In 2012 approximately 1,500 development partnerships have been initiated. Once initiated a project is eligible for public support worth up to € 200,000. [178, 179, 180]

---

[174] Jaffee 2012, p. 94
[175] Raynolds 2012, p. 282
[176] Raynolds 2012, p. 283
[177] Haupt 2006, p. 28
[178] Bahri 2011, p. 3
[179] SCHMIDT et al. 2012, p. 135
[180] SCHMIDT et al. 2012, p. 136

Figure 28: Benefits and common goals in development partnerships (between German development cooperation and the private sector) [181]

The basic benefits and common goals in development partnerships are illustrated in the figure above, but to gain access to this programme, the applying companies have to comply some requirements. The company must have an annual turnover of at least € 1 million, needs to have more than ten employees and three years of market presence. Also all project measures have to meet the development goals and objectives of the German Government, public and private contributions have to complement each other, competitive neutrality must be ensured and even criteria have to be met. [182]

The number of approximately 1,500 development partnerships gives evidence, that there are enough companies that are willing to invest and enable development in producing countries. An example is the project "Wild coffee from Ethiopia". The project was active from 2010 until 2014 and its goal was to improve the contribution of farmers/crofters into the supply chain of certified wild coffee and other products like medical plants and honey to raise the income of

---

[181] SCHMIDT et al. 2012, p. 136
[182] SCHMIDT et al. 2012, pp. 135–136

the population and to preserve the diversity of the rain forest in a long run. The outcome of the project is that more than 60,000 people have a share on the sustainable economic development of the Kafa region through commercialization of wild coffee. International trading companies can rely on a stabilized supply chain and that diversity of the rain forest is protected through a sustainable agriculture.[183]

With regard to the listed possibilities and the appendices there are several possibilities for German coffee producers to plan, fund and execute projects in coffee producing countries in cooperation with German associations, foundations, institutes and the German government to impact the conditions along the coffee supply chain to the effect that the quality, the quantity and the sustainability of the coffee can be increased as well as the conditions for all participants.

[183] Wolf, Hammerstein 2015, p. 2

5   Conclusion and outlook

Coffee, as one of the most consumed drinks in the western hemisphere, is not only an enjoyment, but also an important economic factor. With a total production of 111.1 million 60-kg bags in 2012/2013, worth about US$ 19 billion, it provides employment for hundreds of million people worldwide. The major part of these people are farmers and workers in the producing countries. However coffee also represents a significant economic value for the EU and especially for Germany, as German coffee producers are responsible for the majority of the re-exported coffee worldwide. At the same time, climate change and global warming are proceeding with increasing speed and intensity. As the global temperature increased by an average of 0.74 °C in the period 1906 to 2005, the global temperature is estimated to increase between 1.8 °C and 4.0 °C until the end of this century. Considering these data, there is an ominous risk that large crop areas of *C. arabica* are rendered unsuitable for the production of *C. arabica* coffee.

Given the fact that climate change is affecting the production areas in a negative way, in order to avoid losses and to stabilise the green coffee production the parties involved have to act in time. In this context this research has the goal to indicate the climate change related changes on the global green coffee market in order to derivate approaches for German coffee producers to assure their coffee procurement for the future. This task has been realised with extrapolations of previous data of supply and demand as well as a calculation concerning the loss of *C. arabica* crop areas and *C. arabica* yields until 2050.

The main finding of this study is that the *C. arabica* supply in 2050 can only meet a fraction of the demands. Namely, the calculated *C. arabica* demand worldwide will be at 169.053 thousand 60-kg bags *C. arabica* coffee whilst the yield/supply is expected to be at 43.966 thousand 60-kg bags. This leads to the result that only 26.01 % of the worldwide *C. arabica* demand can be satisfied. Therefore the adaptation of the actual procurement strategies and approaches to mitigate the negative impacts is highly recommended.

As described in chapter 4.2, some approaches like shade management and preventing soil erosion can be realised in a shorter time and with lower costs as they are rather simple. Realising approaches, like the water efficiency, are requiring both, time and funding, on a larger scale, because the farmers and workers have to be trained and for example the UAHR needs to be assembled, shipped and installed. The approaches with the largest impacts, like the breeding of new varieties, the extended usage of Fair Trade certified products as well as micro financing and development aid, require more time and even larger amounts of money to be realized, whilst having a larger risk of failure. Therefore it is not wise for a single company to initialise a large project on its own, especially considering that most actors in the German coffee business are small and medium-sized enterprises.

A new basic concept is needed to maximize the influence and the share of ownership along the supply chain and to minimize the financial risks for a single company. This could increase the chance of success and would help to implement and realize the approaches with the largest impact, like breeding of new varieties. An example for a basic concept could be an association between a lion's share of all the German coffee producing companies, guided under a protectorate like the German Coffee Association, whose members are represented along the whole value added chain (besides the farmers).

The selection which approaches should be used, must not only be based on obvious monetary and economic factors. When some parts of the supply chain are not considered whilst investing, this part of the supply chain can develop into a bottleneck. As it is already apparent that the production, the foundation of the supply chain, will develop into a bottleneck over time, it can be concluded that investments should be focused on this part of the supply chain. Furthermore the best approach for a sustainable stabilisation and extension of the supply chain would be a mixture of environmental, economic and socially sustainable approaches linked to the goal to produce an adequate amount of *C. arabica* coffee in the year 2050 to cover the demand as good as possible. This would also assure that the interests of most stakeholders are considered. If these approaches would be implemented successfully on a large scale, the impact could help saving thousands of jobs in the producing countries, as well as in Europe and Germany and ensure a continuative production of *C. arabica* coffee.

To make decisions where and how to invest in what kind of approach and to evaluate the impacts of the different approaches further research on this topic is needed.

6   Discussion

This thesis is based on secondary literature, so the data used for calculations come from different people or organisations and were evaluated at different points of time. This leads to differences within the collected data. Nevertheless usage of these data for this thesis is essential to create a possible outlook on the coffee balance in 2050 under certain circumstances and to display a foundation for the derivation of procurement strategy alternatives.

The used methods where simple regressions and extrapolations due to average annual growth rates. The available data of supply and demand are based on the past and mostly made up in volumes per year. Whereas the supply data are also influenced by several independent variables like the weather, different soils, farming techniques and fertilisation, the demand data are dependent on exchange fluctuations, crises and the supply. Given that the independent variables cannot be properly calculated in a mathematical way, direct numbers from the literature where needed for the results. The choice to use simple linear regressions and extrapolations due to AAGR's provided by the literature were not only the simplest way to create a possible outlook, it also the most adequate and useful way to forecast these data. This is backed by Armstrong who compared the accuracy of different extrapolation methods in forecasting and states: "Relatively simple extrapolation methods [...] are adequate. [...] These methods provide accuracy equivalent to more complex methods at a lower cost, and they are easier to understand."[184] Also in an expert survey titled "Expert opinions about extrapolation and the mystery of the overlooked discontinuities" by Collopy et al. in 1992 the result was, that the most useful forecasting method is the simple regression[185].

The calculation of the supply of C. arabica for 2050 is also slightly irregular. Because of non-accessible data it was necessary to calculate the actual C. arabica crop area in ha. The data available were the amounts of 60-kg bags of

---

[184] Armstrong 1984, p. 56
[185] Collopy, Armstrong 1992, p. 576

C. arabica which were produced in the countries in 2013(USDA) as well as the crop yield in kg per ha of 2013 (FAO) [186, 187]. This leads to a source of error because the crop yield in kg per ha is for all produced coffee breeds (*C. arabica* and *C. canephora*) in the countries. Nevertheless this is the most logical and approximate approach to calculate the crop area in ha of *C. arabica* for further calculations.

The next possible source of error is in calculation (4) in which the "crop areas in ha per country" where multiplied with the "average mean suitability by region in % of current suitability". Bunn et al. (2014) used the five GCMs from the 5th assessment report of the IPCC (2013) as the foundation of their calculations. Unfortunately they just described their outcome as "[...] relative suitability by 2050 for coffee regions [...]", the data cannot be assigned explicit to the year 2013 or 2014. This could lead to a minor discrepancy in the final result. [188]

Calculation (5) which calculates the expected crop yield for the year 2050 out of the decreased crop area per country and the crop yield in kg per ha has a certain weakness. Taking into consideration that the crop yield is influenced by parameters like environmental changes, abiotic stresses, like extreme temperatures, the soil and the available nutrients, shade and even mycorrhizal fungal spores, it is obvious that the crop yield will definitely change within the 37 years. But at this point the data from 2013 are the only country-specific crop yield data available, it is the best approach do get useful results. [189, 190, 191, 192]

Calculation (7) deals with the estimated coffee demand for the traditional importing countries for 2050 and extrapolates the consumption data of 2012 with an adapted AAGR of 0.5 %. Taking into account that the AAGR for the

---

[186] Food and Agriculture Organization of the United States (FAO) 2015, p. 1
[187] United States Department of Agriculture (USDA) 2014a, p. 1
[188] Bunn et al. 2014b, p. 6
[189] Cardoso et al. 2003, pp. 40–42
[190] Camargo, Marcelo Bento Paes de 2010, pp. 244–245
[191] DaMatta, Ramalho, José D. Cochicho, p. 56
[192] International Coffee Organisation (ICO) 2014, pp. 20–21

period 1964 to 1989 was at 1.3 % and the AAGR for the period 1990 to 2012 was at 0.7 %. Although the population is increasing, the latest low growth rates can be explained by a shrinking average consumption per capita. But to pursue the downward trend whilst considering that the growth was never retrogressive, the author decided to calculate with an adapted and assumed AAGR of 0.5 %. [193]

Another calculation that is impacted by a lack of information is formula (9).The coffee demand of China for the period 2012 to 2020 is calculated with the AAGR of 12.8 %, provided by ICO[194], as the Chinese coffee consumption is expected to rise this quickly. The period 2020 to 2050 is, as the rest of the countries demands, calculated with an AAGR of 4.7 %, which represents the average annual growth of the last years and is expected to continue on this scale[195]. These AAGR's are, like the others, are very vague as the demand also is influenced by the supply and other factors. But as in calculation (7), these AAGR's are the most suitable approach to forecast the demands.

Maybe the biggest source of error can be found in calculation (14), where the simple linear regression for "*C. arabica* share in the year (t)" is calculated. When a simple linear regression is used for forecasting, the period under review should be on a longer scale than the period of forecasting to guarantee a reliable forecast. But as the period under review is 4 years and the period of forecasting is 40 years, the data is not reliable. It can be estimated that the demand will shift more to *C. canephora* as calculated, because the supply is influencing the demand and the supply of *C. arabica* will definitively drop.

Considering the given sources of errors it has to be assumed that the calculated foundation for the derivation of procurement strategy alternatives of German coffee producers is not able to represent the exact forecast of the *C. arabica* supply and demand for 2050. Nevertheless, as this issue is also in the focus of other studies and the major coffee organisations and associations, it can be

---

[193] International Coffee Organisation (ICO) 2014, p. 13
[194] International Coffee Organisation (ICO) 2013b, p. 10
[195] International Coffee Organisation (ICO) 2014, p. 13

agreed that the calculation represents an acceptable assumption of the situation in 2050 and therefore can be used as the foundation for further conclusions[196, 197, 198, 199, 200, 201, 202, 203, 204, 205, 206, 207, 208, 209].

Chapter 4.2 deals with a selection of possible approaches to improve several contact points along the whole coffee supply chain. Not all approaches are concerning procurement strategy alternatives, most of the approaches are focussing on improving existing parts of the supply chain to assure and develop the productivity in a sustainable way. The only approach, which is a direct procurement strategy alternative, is the fair trade approach, which differs from the conventional procurement strategy. Nonetheless, the outcome of this thesis, as it is proposing a combination of different approaches to improve, stabilize and develop the coffee supply chain, offers the German coffee producers an alternative to act against the climate change related changes on the global green coffee market.

[196] Baca et al. 2014
[197] Bariyo 2015
[198] Bunn et al. 2014a
[199] Camargo, Ângelo paes de, Camargo, Marcelo Bento Paes de 2001
[200] Davis et al. 2012
[201] European Coffee Federation (ECF) 2014
[202] Gay et al. 2006
[203] Haggar, Schepp 2012
[204] IPCC 2013
[205] Läderach et al. 2013
[206] Mayer 2013
[207] Nelson et al. 2010
[208] Schroth et al. 2009
[209] Schroth et al. 2014

7   Appendum

Shortly before this thesis was finished two new studies where published that also warn about the possible impact of rising temperatures on the production of *C. arabica* coffee. Unfortunately they could not be considered anymore for the calculations in this thesis.

The study by Alessandro Craparo titled "Coffea arabica yields decline in Tanzania due to climate change: Global implications", which will be published on 15 July 2015 in "Agricultural and Forest Meteorology" Volume 208 describes that climate change is already having an impact on the *C. arabica* production in East African Highland regions. Over the last 49 years the +1.42 °C increase in night temperatures led to a yield decrease of 195 kg/ha which represents losses of 46 %. [210]

The study by Ovalle-Rivera, Läderach et al., titled "Projected Shifts in Coffea arabica Suitability among Major Global Producing Regions Due to Climate Change" and published on the 14 April 2015 focuses on the global impact of climate change towards the suitability of *C. arabica* and comes to a conclusion that confirms the outcome of this study: "Here we have highlighted the global dimension and scale of climate change with its pronounced variation of impacts on Arabica producer countries at regional, continental, and global scales. These show that adaptation strategies are required at all levels. [...] Overall there will be a need for high-quality varieties of Arabica coffee that are better adapted to higher temperatures. This must be a priority for plant breeders in the coming decades. Our global analysis provides a broad classification of countries as either severely or less severely affected by climate change. In terms of production of Arabica coffee, however, each region, and each country within it, will itself be a mosaic of situations. Some areas will become more suitable while others will lose suitability. This calls for approaches at the local scale to help farmers to adapt to climate change." [211]

---

[210] Craparo et al. 2015, pp. 8–9
[211] Ovalle-Rivera et al. 2015, pp. 11–12

8   Publication bibliography

Armstrong, J. Scott (1984): Forecasting by extrapolation: Conclusions from 25 years of research. In *Interfaces* 14 (6), pp. 52–66. Available online at http://core.ac.uk/download/pdf/9311228.pdf, checked on 5/5/2015.

Asian Development Bank (ADB) (2013): What is Climate Change? Available online at http://gms-wga.org/wp-content/uploads/2014/12/bio-brief2l_TA7833_climate_change_LAO_2013.pdf, checked on 2/11/2015.

Baca, María; Läderach, Peter; Haggar, Jeremy; Schroth, Götz; Ovalle, Oriana (2014): An integrated framework for assessing vulnerability to climate change and developing adaptation strategies for coffee growing families in Mesoamerica. In *PloS one* 9 (2), pp. 1–11. DOI: 10.1371/journal.pone.0088463. Available online at http://www.ncbi.nlm.nih.gov/pubmed/24586328, checked on 3/4/2015.

Bahri, Girum (2011): Formulation of criteria for Public Private Partnerships: Considerations to advance environmental and social innovation. Available online at http://gsbblogs.uct.ac.za/gsbconference/files/2011/11/girum-bahri-giz-fragile-states-ppp-criteria-16-08-2011b.pdf, checked on 4/23/2015.

Bariyo, Nicholas (2015): Coffee Consumption Expected to Jump. Edited by The Wall Street Journal. Available online at http://www.wsj.com/articles/coffee-consumption-expected-to-jump-1424119985, checked on 2/17/2015.

Bitzer, Verena; Francken, Mara; Glasbergen, Pieter (2008): Intersectoral partnerships for a sustainable coffee chain: Really addressing sustainability or just picking (coffee) cherries? (2). DOI: 10.1016/j.gloenvcha.2008.01.002. Available online at http://www.sciencedirect.com/science/article/pii/S0959378008000137, checked on 2/7/2015.

Bunn, Christian; Läderach, Peter; Ovalle Rivera, Oriana; Kirschke, Dieter (2014a): A bitter cup: climate change profile of global production of Arabica and Robusta coffee (1-2). DOI: 10.1007/s10584-014-1306-x. Available online at http://link.springer.com/article/10.1007%2Fs10584-014-1306-x, checked on 3/16/2015.

Bunn, Christian; Läderach, Peter; Ovalle Rivera, Oriana; Kirschke, Dieter (2014b): A bitter cup: climate change profile of global production of Arabica and Robusta coffee -Supplementary Material (1-2). DOI: 10.1007/s10584-014-1306-x. Available online at http://static-content.springer.com/esm/art%3A10.1007%2Fs10584-014-1306-x/MediaObjects/10584_2014_1306_MOESM1_ESM.docx, checked on 3/16/2015.

Camargo, Ângelo paes de; Camargo, Marcelo Bento Paes de (2001): Definição e esquematização das fases fenológicas do cafeeiro arábica nas condições tropicais do Brasil (1). Available online at http://www.scielo.br/pdf/brag/v60n1/a08v60n1.pdf, checked on 2/15/2015.

Camargo, Marcelo Bento Paes de (2010): The impact of climatic variability and climate change on arabic coffee crop in Brazil (1). DOI: 10.1590/S0006-87052010000100030. Available online at http://www.scielo.br/scielo.php?script=sci_arttext&pid=S0006-87052010000100030&lng=en&nrm=iso&tlng=en, checked on 2/7/2015.

Cardoso, Irene M.; Boddington, Claire; Janssen, Bert H.; Oenema, Oene; Kuyper, Thomas W. (2003): Distribution of mycorrhizal fungal spores in soils under agroforestry and monocultural coffee systems in Brazil (1). DOI: 10.1023/A:1025479017393. Available online at http://link.springer.com/article/10.1023/A:1025479017393, checked on 4/17/2015.

Carter, Craig R.; Rogers, Dale S. (2008): A framework of sustainable supply chain management: moving toward new theory. Available online at http://www.emeraldinsight.com/doi/abs/10.1108/09600030810882816, checked on 2/7/2015.

Central Intelligence Agency (CIA) (2014): The World Factbook. Available online at https://www.cia.gov/library/publications/the-world-factbook/geos/mx.html, updated on 9/8/2014, checked on 2/17/2015.

Closs, David J.; Speier, Cheri; Meacham, Nathan (2011): Sustainability to support end-to-end value chains: the role of supply chain management (1). DOI: 10.1007/s11747-010-0207-4. Available online at http://link.springer.com/article/10.1007%2Fs11747-010-0207-4, checked on 2/7/2015.

Colbert, Ross (2013): Rabobank Report: Global Beverage Outlook 2013 – Thirsting for Growth. Rabobank. Available online at https://www.rabobank.com/en/press/search/2013/Rabobank_Report_Global_Beverage_Outlook_2013_T hirsting_for_Growth.html, checked on 2/7/2015.

Collopy, Fred; Armstrong, J.Scott (1992): Expert opinions about extrapolation and the mystery of the overlooked discontinuities (4). DOI: 10.1016/0169-2070(92)90067-J. Available online at http://www.sciencedirect.com/science/article/pii/016920709290067J#, checked on 4/29/2015.

Craparo, A.C.W.; van Asten, P.J.A.; Läderach, P.; Jassogne, L.T.P.; Grab, S. W. (2015): Coffea arabica yields decline in Tanzania due to climate change: Global implications. DOI: 10.1016/j.agrformet.2015.03.005. Available online at http://www.sciencedirect.com/science/article/pii/S0168192315000830, checked on 5/1/2015.

DaMatta, Fábio M.; Ramalho, José D. Cochicho: Impacts of drought and temperature stress on coffee physiology and production: a review, vol. 18, pp. 55–81. Available online at http://www.scielo.br/scielo.php?script=sci_arttext&pid=S1677-04202006000100006&lng=en&nrm=iso&tlng=en, checked on 2/7/2015.

Davis, Aaron P.; Gole, Tadesse Woldemariam; Baena, Susana; Moat, Justin (2012): The impact of climate change on indigenous Arabica coffee (Coffea arabica): predicting future trends and identifying priorities. In PloS one 7 (11), pp. 1–13. DOI: 10.1371/journal.pone.0047981. Available online at http://journals.plos.org/plosone/article?id=10.1371/journal.pone.0047981, checked on 2/15/2015.

Deutscher Kaffeeverband (2013): Wert aller Kaffee-Exporte der Anbauländer. Available online at http://www.kaffeeverband.de/images/dkv_inhalte/Presse/Zahlen/international/3-Wertallerexporte.jpg, checked on 1/4/2015.

Deutscher Kaffeeverband (2014): Weltweite Rohkaffee-Exporte nach Sorten. Available online at http://www.kaffeeverband.de/images/dkv_inhalte/Presse/Zahlen/international/4-Weltweiteexsorte.jpg, updated on 6/11/2014, checked on 4/26/2015.

Deutscher Kaffeeverband (2015a): Alle Geschäftskontakte. Available online at
http://www.kaffeeverband.de/kaffeekontakte/geschaeftskontakte/75-
kaffeekontakte/geschaeftskontakte/276-geschaeftskontakte-liste, checked on 5/4/2015.

Deutscher Kaffeeverband (2015b): Der Verband. Available online at http://www.kaffeeverband.de/der-
verband, checked on 5/4/2015.

Dragusanu, Raluca; Giovannucci, Daniele; Nunn, Nathan (2014): The Economics of Fair Trade. In
Journal of Economic Perspectives 28 (3), pp. 217–236. DOI: 10.1257/jep.28.3.217. Available online at
http://www.jstor.org/stable/pdf/23800584.pdf, checked on 4/21/2015.

European Coffee Federation (ECF) (2014): European Coffee Report 2013/2014. European chapter and
key national data. Brüssel. Available online at http://www.ecf-
coffee.org/images/European_Coffee_Report_2013-14.pdf, checked on 2/7/2015.

Food and Agriculture Organization of the United States (FAO) (2014): Erntewert der führenden
Anbauländer von Tee weltweit im Jahr 2012 (in Millionen US-Dollar). Edited by Statista. Available online
at http://de.statista.com/statistik/daten/studie/202111/umfrage/die-10-groessten-teeproduzenten-
weltweit/, updated on 2014, checked on 4/26/2015.

Food and Agriculture Organization of the United States (FAO) (2015): Ernteertrag von Kaffee je Hektar
Anbaufläche nach Anbauländern weltweit im Jahr 2013 (in Kilogramm). Edited by Statista. Available
online at http://de.statista.com/statistik/daten/studie/224792/umfrage/groesste-anbaulaender-fuer-kaffee-
nach-ertrag-pro-hektar/, checked on 4/24/2015.

Gay, C.; Estrada, F.; Conde, C.; Eakin, H.; Villers, L. (2006): Potential Impacts of Climate Change on
Agriculture: A Case of Study of Coffee Production in Veracruz, Mexico. In *Climatic Change* 79 (3-4),
pp. 259–288. DOI: 10.1007/s10584-006-9066-x. Available online at
http://link.springer.com/article/10.1007%2Fs10584-006-9066-x, checked on 2/17/2015.

Giovannucci, Daniele; Ponte, Stefano (2005): Standards as a new form of social contract? Sustainability
initiatives in the coffee industry. In *Food Policy* 30 (3), pp. 284–301. DOI: 10.1016/j.foodpol.2005.05.007.
Available online at http://www.sciencedirect.com/science/article/pii/S030691920500031X, checked on
2/7/2015.

Gitter, Seth R.; Weber, Jeremy G.; Barham, Bradford L.; Callenes, Mercedez; Valentine, Jessa Lewis
(2012): Fair Trade-Organic Coffee Cooperatives, Migration, and Secondary Schooling in Southern
Mexico. In *Journal of Development Studies* 48 (3), pp. 445–463. DOI: 10.1080/00220388.2011.598511.
Available online at
http://www.researchgate.net/profile/Jeremy_Weber/publication/46448399_Fair_Trade-
Organic_Coffee_Cooperatives_Migration_and_Secondary_Schooling_in_Southern_Mexico/links/02e7e5
3566cd89edd4000000.pdf, checked on 4/23/2015.

Greenberg, Russell; Bichier, Peter; Sterling, John (1997): Bird Populations in Rustic and Planted Shade
Coffee Plantations of Eastern Chiapas, Mexico. In *Biotropica* 29 (4), pp. 501–514. DOI: 10.1111/j.1744-
7429.1997.tb00044.x. Available online at http://onlinelibrary.wiley.com/doi/10.1111/j.1744-
7429.1997.tb00044.x/epdf, checked on 4/17/2015.

Analysis of the climate change related changes on the global green coffee market for the
derivation of procurement strategy alternatives of German coffee producers
Page 69

Haddis, Alemayehu; Devi, Rani (2008): Effect of effluent generated from coffee processing plant on the water bodies and human health in its vicinity. In *Journal of hazardous materials* 152 (1), pp. 259–262. DOI: 10.1016/j.jhazmat.2007.06.094. Available online at http://www.sciencedirect.com/science/article/pii/S0304389407009740#, checked on 4/18/2015.

Haggar, Jeremy; Schepp, Kathleen (2012): Coffee and Climate Change. Impacts and options for adaption in Brazil, Guatemala, Tanzania and Vietnam. University of Greenwich (4). Available online at http://www.coffeeandclimate.org/reports_studies.html?file=tl_files/CoffeeAndClimate/Science/Haggar%2 0%26%20Schepp_Impacts%20of%20Climate%20Change%20Synthesis%20Report_ENG.pdf, checked on 12/30/2014.

Hammer, Klaus Jürgen (2013): Mehr als 1 Milliarde Euro Kaffeesteuer 2012 in die Bundeskasse geflossen. Statistisches Bundesamt. Wiesbaden. Available online at https://www.destatis.de/DE/PresseService/Presse/Pressemitteilungen/zdw/2013/PD13_032_p002.html, checked on 2/7/2015.

Haupt, Ulrike (2006): Using microfinance to move out of poverty. In *Agriculture and Rural Development* 1 (2006), pp. 26–29. Available online at http://www.rural21.com/uploads/media/ELR_Microfinance_0106.pdf, checked on 4/27/2015.

Hein, Lars; Gatzweiler, Franz (2006): The economic value of coffee (Coffea arabica) genetic resources. In *Ecological Economics* 60 (1), pp. 176–185. DOI: 10.1016/j.ecolecon.2005.11.022. Available online at http://www.sciencedirect.com/science/article/pii/S0921800905005525, checked on 2/7/2015.

Holmes, Oliver Wendell, Sr. (1891): Over the teacups: Boston: Houghton Mifflin. Available online at http://www.gutenberg.org/files/2689/2689-h/2689-h.htm, checked on 4/28/2015.

Hudson, Mark; Hudson, Ian (2004): Justice, sustainability, and the fair trade movement: A case study of coffee production in Chiapas. In *Social Justice*, pp. 130–146. Available online at http://www.jstor.org/discover/10.2307/29768261?sid=21105805457923&uid=2&uid=67&uid=3&uid=3627 23171&uid=62&uid=5910216&uid=3737864&uid=362723071, checked on 2/7/2015.

International Coffee Organisation (ICO) (2001): DOMESTIC CONSUMPTION CROP YEARS 1990/91 TO 1999/00. Edited by International Coffee Organisation (ICO). Available online at http://dev.ico.org/historical/1990-99/PDF/DOMCONSUMPTION.pdf, checked on 4/24/2015.

International Coffee Organisation (ICO) (2011a): ALL EXPORTING COUNTRIES DOMESTIC CONSUMPTION CROP YEARS 2000/01 TO 2009/10. Edited by International Coffee Organisation (ICO). Available online at http://dev.ico.org/historical/2000-09/PDF/DOMCONSUMPTION.pdf, checked on 4/24/2015.

International Coffee Organisation (ICO) (2011b): Russia. Data for crop/calendar year commencing: 2011. Available online at http://www.ico.org/countries/russia.pdf, checked on 2/11/2015.

International Coffee Organisation (ICO) (2011c): South Africa. Data for crop/calendar year commencing: 2011. Available online at http://www.ico.org/countries/south%20africa.pdf, checked on 2/11/2015.

International Coffee Organisation (ICO) (2013a): Annual Review 2012/13. Edited by International Coffee Organisation (ICO). London. Available online at http://www.ico.org/news/annual-review-2012-13-e.pdf, checked on 2/7/2015.

International Coffee Organisation (ICO) (2013b): Coffee in China. 111th Session. Edited by International Coffee Organisation (ICO). Belo Horizonte. Available online at http://dev.ico.org/documents/cy2012-13/icc-111-8e-study-china.pdf, checked on 2/7/2015.

International Coffee Organisation (ICO) (2013c): Re-exports of coffee by Germany. London. Available online at http://dev.ico.org/documents/cy2012-13/icc-110-4e-re-exports-germany.pdf, checked on 2/9/2015.

International Coffee Organisation (ICO) (2014): WORLD COFFEE TRADE (1963 – 2013): A REVIEW OF THE MARKETS, CHALLENGES AND OPPORTUNITIES FACING THE SECTOR. Edited by International Coffee Organisation (ICO). London. Available online at http://www.ico.org/news/icc-111-5-r1e-world-coffee-outlook.pdf, checked on 2/7/2015.

International Coffee Organisation (ICO) (2015a): #CoffeeTradeStats. Data for crop/calendar year commencing: 2011. Available online at http://www.ico.org/monthly_coffee_trade_stats.asp, checked on 2/11/2015.

International Coffee Organisation (ICO) (2015b): ALL EXPORTING COUNTRIES DOMESTIC CONSUMPTION CROP YEARS 2010/11 TO 2012/13. Edited by International Coffee Organisation (ICO). Available online at http://dev.ico.org/historical/2010-19/PDF/DOMCONSUMP.pdf, checked on 4/24/2015.

International Coffee Organisation (ICO) (2015c): IMPORTS OF ALL FORMS OF COFFEE BY SELECTED IMPORTING COUNTRIES FROM ALL SOURCE DECEMBER 2014. Edited by International Coffee Organisation (ICO). Available online at http://www.ico.org/prices/m4.htm, updated on 3/31/2015, checked on 4/24/2015.

International Coffee Organisation (ICO) (2015d): The Story of Coffee. Available online at http://www.ico.org/coffee_story.asp, checked on 2/6/2015.

International Tea Committee (2014): Erzeugung und Exportvolumen von Tee weltweit in den Jahren 2004 bis 2013 (in Millionen Tonnen). Edited by Statista. Available online at http://de.statista.com/statistik/daten/studie/29841/umfrage/weltproduktion-und-exporte-von-tee-seit-2004/, checked on 4/26/2015.

IPCC (2013): Summary for Policymakers. In: Climate Change 2013: The Physical Science Basis. Contribution of Working Group I to the Fifth Assessment Report of the Intergovernmental Panel on Climate Change. With assistance of Stocker, T.F., D. Qin, G.-K. Plattner, M. Tignor, S.K. Allen, J. Boschung, A. Nauels, Y. Xia, V. Bex and P.M. Midgley. Edited by Cambridge University Press. IPCC. Cambridge, United Kingdom and New York, NY, USA. Available online at http://www.ipcc.ch/pdf/assessment-report/ar5/wg1/WG1AR5_SPM_FINAL.pdf, checked on 4/6/2015.

Jaffee, Daniel (2012): Weak coffee: Certification and co-optation in the fair trade movement. In *Social Problems* 59 (1), pp. 94–116. Available online at

http://www.pdx.edu/sociology/sites/www.pdx.edu.sociology/files/Soc%20Probs%202012--
Weak%20Coffee--Jaffee%20.pdf, checked on 4/21/2015.

Läderach, Peter; Haggar, Jeremy; Lau, Charlotte; Eitzinger, Anton; Ovalle, Oriana; Baca, María et al.
(2013): Mesoamerican coffee: building a climate change adaptation strategy. Edited by CIAT. Available
online at http://biblioteca.catie.ac.cr:5151/repositoriomap/bitstream/123456789/39/3/40.pdf, checked on
2/10/2015.

Lin, Brenda B. (2007): Agroforestry management as an adaptive strategy against potential microclimate
extremes in coffee agriculture. In *Agricultural and Forest Meteorology* 144 (1-2), pp. 85–94. DOI:
10.1016/j.agrformet.2006.12.009. Available online at dx.doi.org/10.1016/j.agrformet.2006.12.009,
checked on 2/7/2015.

Mayer, Amy (2013): Climate Change Already Challenging Agriculture. In *BioScience* 63 (10), pp. 781–
787. DOI: 10.1525/bio.2013.63.10.2. Available online at
http://bioscience.oxfordjournals.org/content/63/10/781, checked on 2/18/2015.

Mondelez International, Inc. (2014): Mondelez International & D.E Master Blenders 1753 to Form
World's Leading Pure-Play Coffee Company. DEERFIELD, Illinois, Amsterdam, Netherlands. Available
online at http://ir.mondelezinternational.com/releasedetail.cfm?releaseid=845966, checked on
4/21/2015.

Murthy, Pushpa S.; Madhava Naidu, M. (2012): Sustainable management of coffee industry by-products
and value addition—A review. In *Resources, Conservation and Recycling* 66, pp. 45–58. DOI:
10.1016/j.resconrec.2012.06.005. Available online at
http://www.sciencedirect.com/science/article/pii/S0921344912000894, checked on 2/7/2015.

Nelson, Gerald C.; Rosegrant, Mark W.; Palazzo, Amanda; Gray, Ian; Ingersoll, Christina; Robertson,
Richard et al. (2010): Food security, farming, and climate change to 2050: Scenarios, results, policy
options: Intl Food Policy Res Inst. Available online at
http://www.ifpri.org/sites/default/files/publications/rr172.pdf, checked on 2/18/2015.

Ovalle-Rivera, Oriana; Läderach, Peter; Bunn, Christian; Obersteiner, Michael; Schroth, Götz (2015):
Projected Shifts in Coffea arabica Suitability among Major Global Producing Regions Due to Climate
Change. In *PloS one* 10 (4), pp. e0124155. DOI: 10.1371/journal.pone.0124155. Available online at
http://journals.plos.org/plosone/article?id=10.1371/journal.pone.0124155, checked on 5/1/2015.

Pachauri, Rajendra K.; Meyer, Leo (2013): CLIMATE CHANGE 2014. Synthesis Report. With assistance
of R.K. Pachauri (Chair), Myles R. Allen (United Kingdom), Vicente Ricardo Barros (Argentina), John.
Intergovernmental panel on climate change. Available online at http://www.ipcc.ch/pdf/assessment-
report/ar5/syr/SYR_AR5_LONGERREPORT.pdf, checked on 12/31/2014.

Phiri, Noah; Baker, Peter (2009): A synthesis of the work of the Regional Coffee Wilt Programme 2000–
2007. Coffee Wilt Disease in Africa. Edited by Commonwealth Agricultural Bureaux International (CABI).
Available online at http://www.common-
fund.org/fileadmin/user_upload/Projects/ICO/ICO_13/Final_Technical_Report_CFC_ICO_13.pdf,
checked on 4/20/2015.

Analysis of the climate change related changes on the global green coffee market for the
derivation of procurement strategy alternatives of German coffee producers
Page 72

Ponte, Stefano (2002): The `Latte Revolution'? Regulation, Markets and Consumption in the Global Coffee Chain. In World Development 30 (7), pp. 1099–1122. DOI: 10.1016/S0305-750X(02)00032-3. Available online at http://www.sciencedirect.com/science/article/pii/S0305750X02000323#, checked on 4/18/2015.

Preibisch, Holger (2012): European Coffee Market with focus on Germany. Deutscher Kaffeeverband. Available online at http://www.eafca.org/wwc/downloads/AFCCE09/presentations/European%20Coffee%20Market%20with%20focus%20on%20Germany%20-%20Holger%20Preibisch.pdf, checked on 4/16/2015.

Raynolds, Laura T. (2012): Fair Trade: Social regulation in global food markets. In Journal of Rural Studies 28 (3), pp. 276–287. DOI: 10.1016/j.jrurstud.2012.03.004. Available online at http://www.sciencedirect.com/science/article/pii/S0743016712000472, checked on 4/21/2015.

SCHMIDT, FABIAN; Wolf, Christine; LAMIK, ANNA KAROLINA; SLUKA, CHARLOTTE (2012): 4.2 working with the private sector: insights from German development cooperation. In Good Business: Making Private Investments Work for Tropical Forests, p. 134. Available online at http://www.profor.info/sites/profor.info/files/docs/ETFRN-54-Good-Business.pdf#page=156, checked on 4/23/2015.

Schroth, Götz; Läderach, Peter; Blackburn Cuero, Diana Sofia; Neilson, Jeffrey; Bunn, Christian (2014): Winner or loser of climate change? A modeling study of current and future climatic suitability of Arabica coffee in Indonesia. In Reg Environ Change, pp. 1–10. DOI: 10.1007/s10113-014-0713-x. Available online at http://link.springer.com/article/10.1007%2Fs10113-014-0713-x, checked on 2/7/2015.

Schroth, Götz; Läderach, Peter; Dempewolf, Jan; Philpott, Stacy; Haggar, Jeremy; Eakin, Hallie et al. (2009): Towards a climate change adaptation strategy for coffee communities and ecosystems in the Sierra Madre de Chiapas, Mexico. In Mitig Adapt Strateg Glob Change 14 (7), pp. 605–625. DOI: 10.1007/s11027-009-9186-5. Available online at http://link.springer.com/article/10.1007%2Fs11027-009-9186-5, checked on 2/7/2015.

Selvamurugan, M.; Doraisamy, P.; Maheswari, M. (2010): An integrated treatment system for coffee processing wastewater using anaerobic and aerobic process. In Ecological Engineering 36 (12), pp. 1686–1690. DOI: 10.1016/j.ecoleng.2010.07.013. Available online at http://www.sciencedirect.com/science/article/pii/S0925857410002211#, checked on 4/18/2015.

Stefanie Schmitt (2015): Kaffee gewinnt in der VR China immer mehr Liebhaber. Germany Trade & Invest. Beijing. Available online at http://www.gtai.de/GTAI/Navigation/DE/Trade/maerkte,did=1165010.html, checked on 2/7/2015.

United States Department of Agriculture (USDA) (2014a): Arabica Coffee Production. Available online at http://apps.fas.usda.gov/psdonline/psdReport.aspx?hidReportRetrievalName=Arabica+Coffee+Production&hidReportRetrievalID=1673&hidReportRetrievalTemplateID=8, checked on 2/24/2015.

United States Department of Agriculture (USDA) (2014b): Coffee: World Markets and Trade. Washington. Available online at http://apps.fas.usda.gov/psdonline/circulars/coffee.pdf, checked on 2/7/2015.

Vermeulen, Sonja J.; Challinor, Andrew J.; Thornton, Philip K.; Campbell, Bruce M.; Eriyagama, Nishadi; Vervoort, Joost M. et al. (2013): Addressing uncertainty in adaptation planning for agriculture. In *Proceedings of the National Academy of Sciences of the United States of America* 110 (21), pp. 8357–8362. DOI: 10.1073/pnas.1219441110. Available online at http://www.ncbi.nlm.nih.gov/pubmed/23674681, checked on 2/18/2015.

Wolf, Christine; Hammerstein, Florian (2015): Wildkaffee Anbau in Äthiopien. Eine Chance für Kleinbauern und die biologische Vielfalt der Region Kafa. Edited by Deutsche Gesellschaft für Internationale Zusammenarbeit (GIZ) GmbH. Available online at http://www.developpp.de/sites/default/files/developpp_factsheet_original_food_de_02-02-2015_final.pdf, checked on 4/23/2015.

World Meteorological Organization (WMO) (2008): World Climate News. The IPCC Fourth Assessment Report. Available online at http://www.wmo.int/pages/prog/www/WIS/Publications/WCN32_final_E.pdf, checked on 2/15/2015.

9   Appendices

Appendix 1: Suitability changes by the 2050s in the RCP 2.6 scenario; A-D: Arabica, E-G: Robusta. Hatching indicates the current suitability distribution; Warm colors represent areas with negative climate change impacts and cold colors positive changes[212]

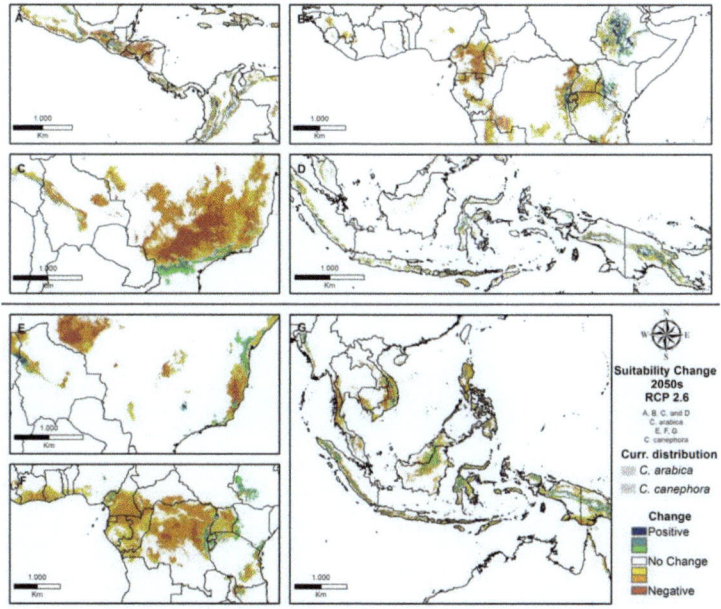

[212] Bunn et al. 2014b, p. 3

Appendix 2: Suitability changes by the 2050s in the RCP 8.5 scenario; A-D: Arabica, E-G: Robusta. Hatching indicates the current suitability distribution; Warm colors represent areas with negative climate change impacts and cold colors positive changes[213]

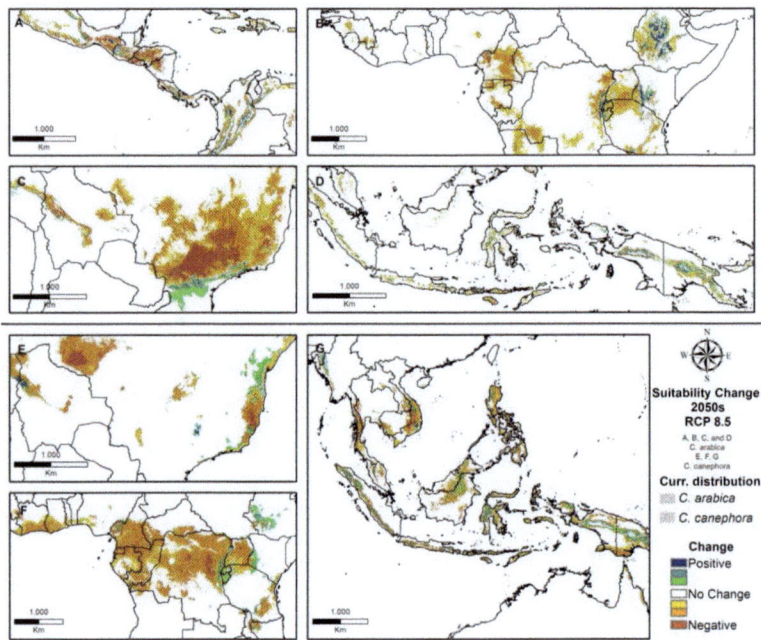

---

[213] Bunn et al. 2014b, p. 4

Appendix 3: Calculation *C. arabica* production for 2050

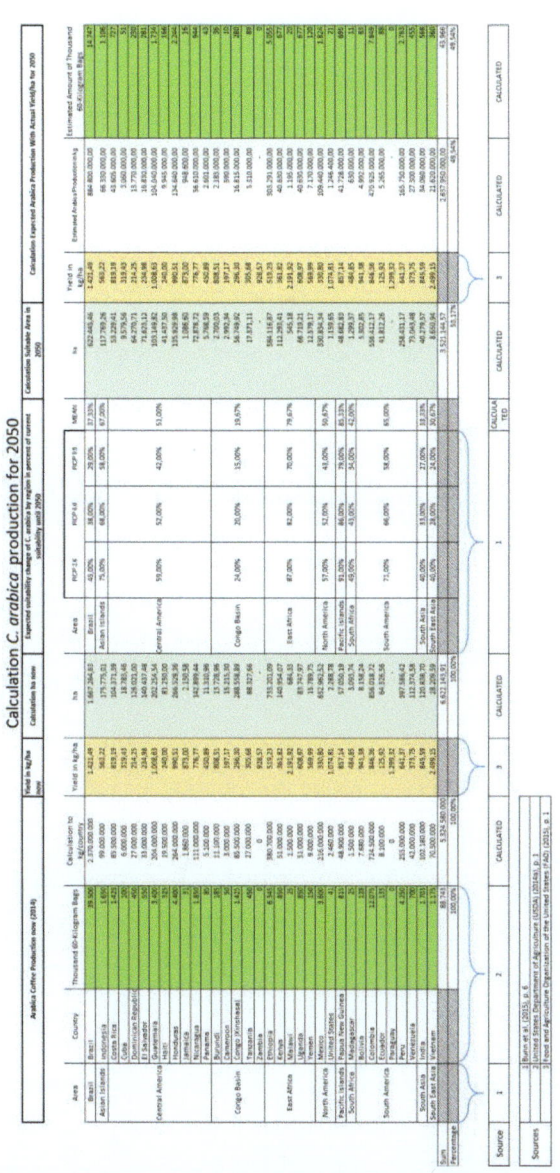

Analysis of the climate change related changes on the global green coffee market for the
derivation of procurement strategy alternatives of German coffee producers
Page 77

Appendix 4: Calculation total coffee demand (*C. arabida* and *C. canephora*) for 2050

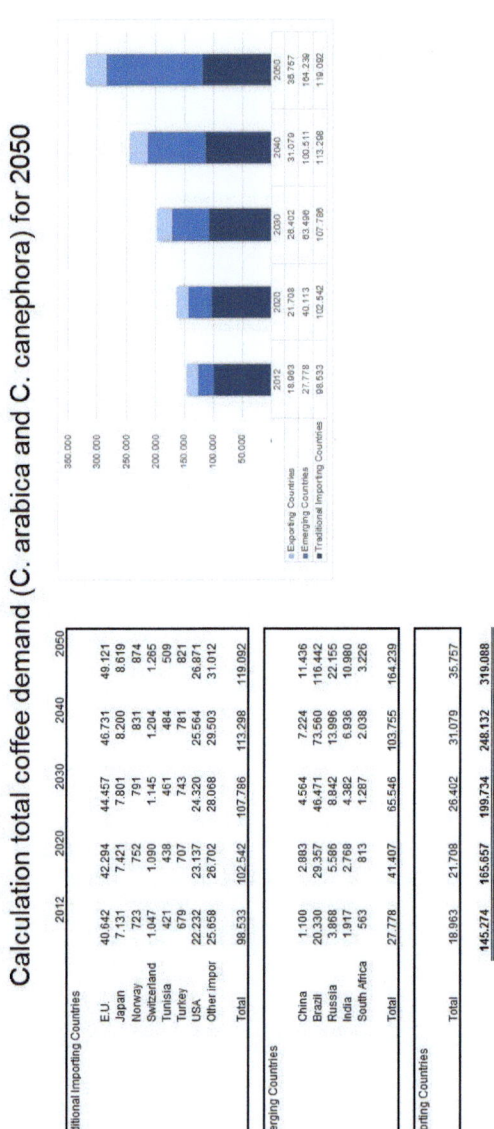

Calculation total coffee demand (C. arabica and C. canephora) for 2050

	2012	2020	2030	2040	2050
Traditional Importing Countries					
E.U.	40.642	42.294	44.457	46.731	49.121
Japan	7.131	7.421	7.801	8.200	8.619
Norway	723	752	791	831	874
Switzerland	1.047	1.090	1.145	1.204	1.265
Tunisia	421	438	461	484	509
Turkey	679	707	743	781	821
USA	22.232	23.137	24.320	25.564	26.871
Other impor	25.658	26.702	28.068	29.503	31.012
Total	98.533	102.542	107.786	113.298	119.092
Emerging Countries					
China	1.100	2.883	4.564	7.224	11.436
Brazil	20.330	29.357	46.471	73.560	116.442
Russia	3.868	5.586	8.842	13.996	22.155
India	1.917	2.768	4.382	6.936	10.980
South Africa	563	813	1.287	2.038	3.226
Total	27.778	41.407	65.546	103.755	164.239
Exporting Countries					
Total	18.963	21.708	26.402	31.079	35.757
	145.274	165.657	199.734	248.132	319.088

Analysis of the climate change related changes on the global green coffee market for the
derivation of procurement strategy alternatives of German coffee producers
Page 78

Appendix 5: Damage costs for three major coffee pests (all costs in 1000 US$)[214]

Continent	Coffee berry dis.		Meloidogyne spp.		Coffee rust		Total damage costs
	Crop losses	Damage costs	Crop losses (%)	Damage costs	Crop losses (%)	Damage costs	
Africa	30%	228,456	5	35,229	6	55,086	318,771
South America	–		12	563,480	13	724,271	1,287,751
Central America	–		10	171,112	10	233,334	404,446
Asia	–		9	34,767	10	50,336	85,103
Total		228,456		804,589		1,063,027	2,096,072

Note: damage costs include crop losses, costs of pesticides and labor costs associated with pesticide application. Coffee production data are from USDA (2004) and FAOSTAT (2004); coffee losses are from Zentmyer and Schieber (1984), Oerke et al. (1994), Kushalappa and Eskes (1989), Anzueto et al. (2001) and Van der Vossen (2001). Pesticide costs are from De Graaff (1986), Kushalappa and Eskes (1989); and Oerke et al. (1994). Full data and calculations are available from the authors.

---

[214] Hein, Gatzweiler 2006, p. 179

Appendix 6: Characteristics of coffee chain restructuring (governance structure and institutional framework)[215]

	ICA regime (1962–89)	Post-ICA regime (1989-present)
Geography of production	At first concentrated in few large producing countries (Brazil, Colombia); later, increasingly dispersed with the emergence of new producers	Fragmentation continues
Entry barriers to production	Low, due to government intervention (input and credit supply, extension, coffee cultivation campaigns, price stabilization)	Increased, due to government withdrawal from the provision of services to farmers (end of input supply schemes, breakdown of research and extension networks, end of price stabilization mechanisms)
Characteristics of internationally traded product	Relatively homogeneous, but distinguished by physical and intrinsic qualities (the latter especially for Mild Arabica)	Bifurcated trend: increased homogenization of lower quality coffees, especially Robusta (bulk export in containers without bags); at the same time, increased trade of small quantities of specific high-end-quality beans (Mild Arabica)
Entry barriers to trade	*Domestic trade and export*: high barriers due to monopoly of marketing or politically set domestic trade quotas *International trade*: increasing due to consolidation	*Domestic trade and export*: first, decreased entry barriers due to liberalization; later, increased barriers following the strengthening of international trader operations in producing countries *International trade*: increasing entry barriers in "fair-average-quality" market due to further consolidation and requirements set by roasters through SMI; decreasing in the specialty market due to fragmentation and the growing importance of e-commerce sales
Distribution of total income generated along the chain	Relatively stable, with farmers getting around 20% of the total, and consuming country operators around 50%	Shifted to the advantage of consuming country operators
Geography of consumption	Concentrated in North America, Western Europe and Japan	Emergence of new markets (Eastern Europe, China, East Asia)
Typology of consumption	Segmented by group of countries (different coffee types and blends catering for the USA/UK markets, Southern Europe, Scandinavia, Central Europe, Japan), but relatively homogeneous consumption within these geographical areas	*Increased fragmentation*: multiplication of types of product and blurring of distinctive lines of preference between different groups of countries; increasing importance of "single origin" coffees

---

[215] Ponte 2002, p. 1113

Appendix 7: Characteristics of coffee chain restructuring (input–output structure and geographies of production and consumption)[216]

	ICA regime (1962–89)	Post-ICA regime (1989-present)
Governance structure of the chain	Low level of "drivenness;" increasing concentration in roasting and trading segments raises entry barriers, but roasters are neither in the position to dictate the terms of the trade to traders, nor to set inclusion/exclusion thresholds; control over the chain by any actor is limited	"Buyer-driven" (specifically, roaster-driven); further consolidation in roasting; oversupply; adoption of SMI by roasters forces traders to integrate upstream; vertical integration by traders made easier by market liberalization in producing countries
Vertical integration	Not common; sometimes occurring in export/international trade links; more rarely into domestic trade and processing	Increasing; international traders integrate into export, processing, domestic trade and sometimes even estate production; vertical integration much more limited in the roaster-international trader link
Producer–consumer country relations	In relative equilibrium; mediated through the ICAs	Absence of formalized relations; consuming country domination
Institutional framework (international)	*Strong*: international trade regulated by ICAs	*Weak*: end of ICA; producing country cartels fail to set up effective quota or retention schemes; futures market increasingly de-linked from market fundamentals
Institutional framework (domestic)	*Strong*: markets monopolized by marketing boards, or regulated by stabilization funds and quasi-governmental producer associations	*Weak*: government and quasi-government institutions retreat into oversight functions or are eliminated altogether; trade associations fill only part of the formal institutional vacuum
Quality conventions	*International-level*: product-based; set in negotiation with producing-country sellers (and/or marketing boards) and maintained via instrument-based testing and inspection, cup testing, and certification of the product; in general, quality assessed by the buyer *ex-post* *Domestic-level*: set by a regulatory agency; includes specific quality control procedures along the chain	*International-level*: increasing importance of conventions defined by buyers; process monitoring (in addition to product testing) becomes important for fair trade, organic, shade-grown coffees; quality increasingly assessed by buyers *ex-ante* *Domestic-level*: increasingly set by buyers; formal rules of quality control remain but are increasingly disregarded
Upgrading possibilities	Limited; undifferentiated trade; however, producing countries achieve product valorization through higher international prices provided by the ICA	Potentially increasing through marketing of "conscious" coffee and direct e-commerce sales; openings in specialty markets more suitable to estates than smallholders

---

[216] Ponte 2002, p. 1112

Appendix 8: Educational sustainability categories[217]

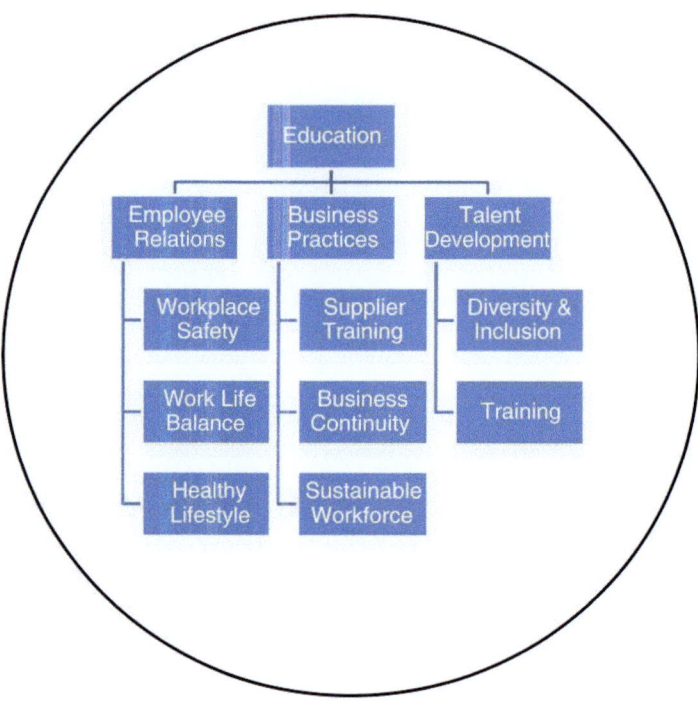

[217] Closs et al. 2011, p. 113

Analysis of the climate change related changes on the global green coffee market for the
derivation of procurement strategy alternatives of German coffee producers
Page 82